Comparative
Political
Analysis

Comparative Political Analysis

Allan L. Larson

Nelson-Hall *nh* Chicago

Library of Congress Cataloging in Publication Data

Larson, Allan L
    Comparative political analysis.

Bibliography: p.
    Includes index.
        1. Comparative government.   I.   Title.
JF51.L37   320.3   79–16862
ISBN 0–88229–257–9 (cloth)
ISBN 0–88229–729–5 (paper)

Manufactured in the United States of America

10   9   8   7   6   5   4   3   2   1

This book is lovingly dedicated
to my father and to the memory
of my mother (1910–1977), my first and best teachers.

Contents

Acknowledgments

The indebtedness that I have incurred during the gestation of this book makes me shrink from the task of singling out individuals. Colleagues, students, friends, and relatives have helped in various ways. All of the members of the Department of Political Science at Loyola University of Chicago have played an important role in my professional life. Certainly, the book owes a great deal to the undergraduate and graduate students who it has been my privilege to teach at Loyola.

I must acknowledge the three chairmen under whose leadership I have pursued my study. Joseph F. Small, S. J., Thomas J. Bennett, and Sam C. Sarkesian have each created an atmosphere in which productive scholarly work could be accomplished.

I am grateful to the following people for help and encouragement: Victor G. Rosenblum, R. Barry Farrell, Charles Marshall, Ronald E. Walker, Francis J. Yartz, Edward J. Crane, Theodore W. Loeppert, Mildred I. Rauch, Clem Aita, Jr., Peter G. Kokalis, Yi-Chun Chang, Carl R. Kannewurf, Robert Haag, C. Gray Bream, Matthew W. Stefanich, Jr., Dorothy Anderson, Phyllis Oman, and Terri Dawn Craven.

My greatest debt is to my sister, Marlys Larson. She has contributed so much in so many ways that I am pleased to be able to express my gratitude in a formal fashion. Perhaps most important, she has been there to remind me that there are more momentous things in life than the study of politics.

Any errors in fact or interpretation are mine alone.

ONE

The Scope of Comparative Political Analysis

The study of comparative government is as old as political science. All the classical works on political theory were based essentially on a comparative approach. Comparative politics claims Aristotle as its founding father. Before embarking on his *Politics,* Aristotle collected and carefully analyzed 158 constitutions of the Greek world of his day. Tó both Plato and Aristotle, politics was the master science; they could conceive of nothing more important, because politics pervaded every aspect of life in the Greek city-state. Remarkably, the problems raised by Aristotle and the methods he employed are similar to those still current in political analysis.

From Aristotle there stretches a long line of other great political thinkers who have given us new perspectives for observing the fascinating variety of political systems which have existed in human history. The collective experiences of mankind provide the problems and the phenomena for those parallel comparisons which students of comparative politics attempt to elaborate. Since the political life of mankind has been exceedingly rich and varied, we are blessed with an embarrassment of riches in our attempts to compare, classify, and criticize past and present political systems.

Since ancient times, men have marveled at the diversity of political systems and governmental institutions rooted in various cultures and societies. Scholars have struggled to bring some degree of order and intelligent discrimination out of this bewildering variety, since there is no "natural" classification inherent in the systems themselves. The political scientist who studies modern political systems is concerned with the development of schemes of analysis that will be comprehensive and that will include relevant categories for the collection of data.

The study of comparative politics is in a state of flux. During the last two decades, an intellectual revolution has been taking place in that study. Ferment in the field is evident both in the substance of the professional literature and in expressions of opinion within the profession.[1] There has been increasing concern with the interrelationships of structures and processes in the political system as a whole. In particular, there has been a growing interest in carrying out systematic research, using survey data from various countries, to examine cross-national patterns of political behavior.

Inquiry in comparative politics has taken many paths and been influenced by a variety of other intellectual disciplines. The interest in comparative methodology is, no doubt, a highly encouraging phenomenon. Since the mid–1950s, the study of comparative politics has moved toward a general theory of politics.

In the long tradition of political theory, the problem of classifying and differentiating governmental systems has been a central one. But systems and classifications are always tentative; they cannot claim finality. That is why meaningful political analysis is a never ending task, and we can at the very best hope to attain a "probabilistic theory of the polity."[2]

The Nature of Comparative Analysis

To compare is to examine simultaneously similarities and differences. Note that by this definition comparison assumes

---

[1] See Richard L. Merritt, *Systematic Approaches to Comparative Politics* (Chicago: Rand McNally, 1970).

[2] The phrase is used by Gabriel Almond and James Coleman in *The Politics of the Developing Areas* (Princeton: Princeton University Press, 1960).

similarities and differences: one does not compare things which are exactly the same, nor those which are completely different. Comparison requires a certain analogy between the things compared. The difficulty lies in determining the degree of analogy present. A constant danger of the comparative method is the making of artificial comparisons based on distortions of the objects compared. The further removed from one another in space, time, and context the things compared are, the greater are the chances of artificiality.

More specifically, the function of comparative analysis is to identify uniformities and differences and to explain them. Comparative politics is concerned with significant regularities, similarities, and differences in the working of political institutions and in political behavior. In a number of respects, different political systems display very similar characteristics. These empirical regularities occur not only in nation-states but also in social clubs, business firms, cities, and many other political systems.

The data of scientific analysis ultimately rests on observation. However, there are vast areas of scientific endeavor which are entirely rational in character. Logic is applied to science constantly because logic contains the rules of what we recognize as valid thinking. If observation is the base of a science, general laws are its crown. The body of any science is a set of general laws from which the occurrence of particular events can be predicted. Of course, there is neither neatness nor simplicity to the human relations of political association. Because political activity consists of the behavior of thinking and feeling human beings, the conceptual problems of the political scientist are more difficult than those of the natural scientist. Perhaps the most troublesome methodological problem for the student of politics stems from this fact—his subject matter consists of human beings. Whatever else political science may be concerned with, it is certainly concerned, first and foremost, with the behavior of human beings.

In focusing their attention on political man, students of political life raise complex and difficult questions. Moreover, political science deals in the main with the behavior of large numbers of people; it must necessarily place a great emphasis upon man in general. At bottom, all society is both part and product of man's social nature. By stressing the human element, comparative study can avoid the meaningless comparison of empty form and sterile ritual. Human behavior can never be explained solely in terms of the external forces acting upon it; we must always reckon with the human agent himself and with the alternative choices open to him in a given situation.

Science is cumulative in that present knowledge is based on past knowledge. Most of the political knowledge we have accumulated to date is the product of disciplined efforts by many investigators. Scientific conclusions are held tentatively. Science is self-corrective through the continued application of its methods in a successive approximation of truth. As noted earlier, science does not claim absolute truth for any of its conclusions, only probability. All political systems undergo change. Because political relationships and institutions change, we should be on guard against giving too much weight to the conformities of social life or the political institutions they support. Change is constant, and every generalization elaborated will have exceptions to challenge it. In the entire history of political institutions, no political system has ever been immutable.

In the continuing corrective analysis which occupies our efforts, comparative study gives us vantage points which are not only useful but quite indispensable if we are to develop a body of reliable knowledge in the light of which predictions of trends and recommendations of policy can be made. Perhaps this is a good time to emphasize that the comparative study of politics has as its main goal the advancement of knowledge. What is done with this knowledge is not immediately relevant. It can be conceded readily that the findings of any of the social sciences can be employed by anyone and for a great variety of purposes. This is true of all knowledge. Any of the generalizations developed in political science must be considered with full recognition of the quicksand nature of human motivation.

Political man has done and will continue to do many strange things. In the effort to cope with the more enigmatic aspects of human behavior, the primary precaution is to take nothing for granted. "Appearances are deceiving" might be a good motto for the student to adopt as he works his way through the labyrinth of comparative government and politics.

It is our goal to make significant comparisons among political systems; that is, to relate political phenomena found in diverse settings. A minimum requirement for comparison is that it should be based on a conceptual framework that provides a number of interrelated concepts which are capable of being applied uniformly to the cases being compared. One of the fundamental principles of comparison is that there must be complete clarity as to what particular characteristics are being analyzed. Professor Ralph Braibanti states this goal succinctly:

> The ultimate aim of comparative political analysis stated briefly, is: From the experiences of separate political systems in different stages of development and in different cultures, hypotheses of a political process of presumptive universal validity may be verified and from this theories of politics may emerge.[3]

The question of "criteria of relevance" obviously enters at this point. By what method can the political scientist determine how deep to go when dealing with the interrelations of these various factors? There would appear to be no general scientific formula by which to decide this crucial question. Criteria of relevance can be best established through a pragmatic approach in the search for political understanding and explanation. The search for patterns of political activity requires abstraction, because concrete institutions and processes can never be compared as such. When we compare, we inevitably distort the unique and the concrete. Different social scientists find different patterns in the behavior of the same set of people. Each discipline is abstracting from the same concrete reality, selecting those aspects central to its own branch of study. All knowledge is

---

[3] Ralph Braibanti, "Comparative Political Analytics Reconsidered," *The Journal of Politics,* vol. 30 (February 1968), p. 32.

selective. We do violence to reality by dissecting it, but it is only by such dissection that we are able to apprehend reality in meaningful fashion.

Students of comparative analysis must choose their approaches from a very wide assortment of concepts, theories, hypotheses, and substantive data. The final product represents an attempt to arrive at an adequate synthesis of the theory and the empirical data relative to the subject under investigation. A disciplined selection must be made from this vast universe. The various approaches and techniques employed in comparative analysis have substantially different implications for the process of theory-building in the discipline. The "final" product is never a finished product, for the analyst is always "overtaken by events" before the ink is dry on the page.

There are, however, ways to hinder the movement toward obsolescence implicit in the writing of a book on comparative analysis. One can concentrate on the perennial, enduring aspects of the political process and emphasize the continuities which persist in the midst of change. By utilizing this approach, the careful student will not be inundated by disconnected, unrelated facts. Another way to grapple with the problem of rapid erosion of relevance is to employ frameworks of analysis which accentuate the structural and functional relationships obtaining in the political system. We shall present a detailed analysis of the structural-functional approach in a later section of this book. Here it is enough to say that structural-functional analysis describes social reality largely in terms of structures, processes, mechanisms, and functions. The analyst determines the important structures and then attempts to trace the functions of those structures. For instance, the frameworks which David Easton and Gabriel Almond have developed, by which broad theories of political development may be linked with the more traditional analytic schemes of comparative analysis,[4] show considerable promise.

---

[4] See David Easton, *A Systems Analysis of Political Life* (New York: John Wiley and Sons, 1965), for the most complete development of the

The problems of comparative method revolve around the discovery and exploration of uniformities and differences. A mastery of the material in this book will provide a suitable background for further exploration of the many difficult and fascinating problems involved in comparative analysis. It will prove helpful whether directed toward modern Western nation-states or the less fully differentiated non-Western political systems. We shall have more to say on the challenge of cross-cultural political analysis at a later point.

The Language of Comparative Politics

Communication about politics takes place in many different contexts. All branches of the social sciences deal with human actions which occur in infinite variety and change even while being examined. Phenomena of human action, both individual and social, do not submit readily to rigid classification and explicit terminology. Because of this difficulty with social analysis, careful students attempt to elaborate precise, unambiguous concepts to orient their discourse about political life.

Where language does not exist, there remains little that is human. One need only try to visualize a human group trying to get along without language to realize how much it means to mankind as an indispensable medium of communication. Language is the primary condition and factor of human interaction. It reflects every phase and aspect of human life; it largely determines our patterns of thought and action. Politics is talk. Not all talk is politics and politics is not all talk, but the central activity of politics is talking.[5]

The use of language to provide sanctification of action is precisely what makes politics different from other ways of allocating values. That is, it is talk and the response to talk which

---

systems-analysis model. For the progressive development of Gabriel Almond's thought, see the collection of analytical writings in his *Political Development* (Boston: Little, Brown, 1970).

[5] Professor H. Mark Roelofs has written a book devoted to the proposition that politics is a distinctively human activity in which men try to converse about their problems. See his *The Language of Modern Politics: An Introduction to the Study of Government* (Homewood, Ill.: Dorsey Press, 1967).

measures political potency. It is from such talk that political scientists discover the interests, values, and orientations that constitute some of the basic raw material of political situations. Language is a necessary catalyst of politics. The words a group employs can often be taken as an index of group norms. A study of its vocabulary reveals how the group views the political world and the consequences for the political system of their particular perceptions.

Every subject requires a technical vocabulary, whether it is plumbing, philosophy, polo, or political science. To express ideas, words or symbols must be employed. Perhaps new terms must be invented; possibly old terms must be given new slants and twists of meaning. Verbal initiation is required in every academic discipline, so too is continuing creativity in the use of concepts and terminology. The search for a distinctive language has been a constant intellectual activity for social scientists.

Concepts are the language of science. They identify the parts of phenomena which we discriminate from the mass and find significant. A concept is a mental construction, an abstract idea that refers either to a class of phenomena or to certain characteristics a range of phenomena have in common. Concepts are thus abstractions from reality which designate types and classes of phenomena.

When we speak of the British Parliament or of Charles De Gaulle or of the Reichstag fire, our words are specific and concrete. They identify things, persons, or events and thus have only one application. Such words are indispensable, but if we were limited only to them, we could never generalize about human behavior. Hence we resort to the formation of concepts. There are two difficulties involved in this very necessary intellectual activity. On the one hand, the very abstractness of a concept leads to the danger that it may become increasingly remote from the living reality it is designed to explain. When this occurs, a scholar may become obsessed with the logic of the internal consistency of the concept rather than with its correspondence with the facts he is explaining. On the other hand, we must be on our guard against a belief that facts can be organized in a conceptual vacuum. All scientific research is carried on within conceptual frameworks. The development of concepts is a collaborative enterprise within the various academic disciplines.

Comparative political analysis inevitably makes use of many concepts varying greatly in their level of abstraction. The greater the number of phenomena to which a concept relates, the higher its level of abstraction is said to be. Although concepts at every level of abstraction are useful, the higher-level abstractions assert a likeness among greater numbers of phenomena. Although high-level abstractions are potentially more significant in reflecting relationships, their very breadth may lead to a degree of ambiguity and lack of clarity.

Comparative analysis makes use of concepts when it notes likes and unlikes, similarities and differences, and identifies patterns, groups, classes, or combinations of various phenomena. Comparative politics analyzes much data of a concrete nature; it does attempt also to go beyond this level of analysis and think in terms of classes, categories, and types rather than in terms of the multitude of different items involved. Shared characteristics are the very essence of comparative analysis.

We try to conceptualize a subject in ways we hope will yield significant intercorrelations; however, low intercorrelations do not necessarily invalidate a concept. Moreover, concepts are of fundamental importance not only in expressing knowledge but in guiding inquiry when we are seeking knowledge. While theories are thought of primarily as true or false, concepts are more accurately described as applicable or inapplicable, useful or useless, productive or sterile. Concept formation is not a matter of determining what a term "really means," but is rather a matter of describing a certain phenomenon in as general a form as the available data permit and then searching for the term which comes closest to serving as a useful sign to denote this phenomenon. For example, the problem is not what *charisma* really means, in the sense of consulting authorities or a dictionary for a definition, but rather when to employ the concept of *charisma* to describe a recurrent political phenomenon.

Without precise concepts and orderly ways of analyzing and arranging data, the student of comparative politics can be easily overwhelmed by the magnitude of his undertaking. The comparative study of political systems is a difficult intellectual task. To compare political institutions and political behavior without regard to differences in history, culture, and social elements is more likely to open the door to misunderstanding than to enlightenment. For example, the comparison of externals in the study of politics may often prove worse than useless. Institutions which bear the same name can be utterly unlike in their actual functioning. A mere study of the framework of institutions may be quite misleading as to their vitality or real importance.

Human beings sharing common language have a standardized set of concepts denoting similar generalizations about classes of things. We abstract from complex situations and we generalize our abstractions. Concepts lead us to look for patterns, regularities, or uniformities in the world around us. Political scientists are not concerned with the unique but with those repetitive patterns which can be distinguished as we observe the political behavior of mankind. Note, however, that uniqueness or individuality is not denied as a real quality of human existence and behavior.

It is quite true that, in a sense, every phenomenon is unique; every person, every process, every nation embodies a unique quality that resists classification. But the very process of thought, not to mention the possibility of a social science, proceeds by noting certain distinguishable features in things. Our knowledge of things involves abstraction from the infinitely complex and unique properties inherent in social situations. There is no necessary conflict between an interest in the unique and a concern with the repetitive features of human life. Rather, they are alternative ways to pay attention to the world around us.

Political concepts focus attention upon those selected

aspects of reality with which the political scientist is concerned; they distinguish political science from the other social sciences, each of which sees other aspects of the same social phenomena from its own perspective. Concepts in effect tell us what to look for in our approach to specific empirical problems. General concepts lead us to the specific factors relevant to the problems we are analyzing.

A concept of comparative politics is an idea about some aspect of political life. It is an agreement to designate an identified factor with a name. Considerable difference of opinion exists within political science about which concepts should be employed. Unlike fields such as medicine or law, the student of political science is confronted with a degree of terminological disorder and conceptual disagreement which creates confusion and ambiguity in scholarly discourse. Doctors and lawyers have attained a considerable degree of consensus on their vocabulary. Two lawyers in a courtroom have a common cluster of concepts which allow them to communicate with a high degree of precision. Two doctors comparing diagnostic notes on a patient can communicate with considerable facility. Such conceptual agreement does not eliminate disagreement arising from differing interpretations and judgments regarding the application of the concepts, but the basic concepts are not in dispute for most cases that are discussed. In political discourse, there is inconsistency in the use of terminology by various writers describing the same social phenomena. Moreover, the same writer will use a term to refer to different types of social phenomena, sometimes on the same page. Thus there are two hundred fifty or so available definitions of the concept of "culture." Small wonder that scholars might despair of the possibility of a common language of the social sciences.

Actually, the inconsistency and semantic confusion are not a major liability. Straining after a rigid scientific precision may not be as rewarding as it first appears. We have already stated that the growth of any discipline requires a continual testing of the alternative concepts that are offered up for use in the competitive marketplace of ideas. A rigorous refinement of concepts alone will not spur progress in the study of politics.

Emphasis on concepts which already have been formulated may serve to retard the formation of new ones. Concepts may act as blinders; once we have developed a set of concepts, we are likely to see only what they alert us to see. We may fail to observe new phenomena, or we may force new data into the old conceptual framework in a Procrustean manner.

Political relationships and institutions change, but conceptual change may lag behind. There is thus a tyranny in political concepts which is concealed by their utility. Concepts alone do not constitute a discipline. They are the building blocks from which a science is constructed. The process of conceptual analysis and clarification is an inherent and persistent feature of political inquiry. The student of comparative politics should ask if we would really benefit by a distinctive professional language. The question is one which preoccupies a great many political scientists today in most sub-fields of the discipline.

In any case, to have any meaning at all, *politics* must refer to concrete phenomena that occur in human society. No one can say in advance that a particular conceptual framework will certainly produce valuable results. The term *politics* is used to designate a wide range of activities, and to insist upon a "theory of politics" would be as fruitless as to ask for a "theory of biology." Any attempt at exhaustive description and explanation is doomed to failure because of the very nature of the subject matter. In the light of this sobering and humbling truth, we must evaluate any conceptual framework basically in terms of its applications to empirical data. The primary objective of a conceptual framework is to extract meaning from mountains of data and render it intelligible by discerning relationships which might otherwise be obscured. The student of political activities is always confronted with a conceptual problem *and* a body of phenomena, and never just one alone. Concepts stem from the resulting interplay of imagination and observation of empirical data.

There are always assumptions underlying the construction of a conceptual framework which cannot be empirically validated but must be accepted as a first step in the research process. Concepts can be fruitful even when they serve a simple heuristic function; that is, when they stimulate investigation along promising lines of inquiry. Immanuel Kant put the problem cogently: "Nature must be interrogated." The conceptual framework organizes the meaningful questions. It sets forth the categories which will tell us more about our subject matter than if we simply proceeded to collect facts in a random fashion.

One mistake which should be avoided is the temptation to reify abstract concepts as we move along in our study. Reification is the common tendency to speak of abstractions as if they embodied the concrete reality identified by the symbolic representation. We treat the symbolic construct as if it were itself the thing. For example, the term *power* is an abstraction. It is not the name of a thing but of a concept describing a relationship between two or more persons. Power considered as a political concept is not something substantive with positive dimensions in time and space. Concepts of power are symbolic representations for social relationships of command and obedience. Power manifests itself in action, and all of us have felt the *effects* of power. But power itself eludes our grasp for the reason that it is not a substantive thing.

Most important concepts used by political scientists, such as power, are symbols which single out particular aspects of complex phenomena. They should never be reified in the mind of the user in such a way as to predicate the existence of an entity with a life and will of its own, existing independently of the life and will of the human beings who compose it. Many distinguished political writers have reified the state in precisely this fashion. Thus we find so-called "organic" theories of the state in which the writer frequently refers to the "purposes" or the "actions" of the state. Granted that such figurative language is often very convenient, the student of social science should learn to fight the unintended implications of his linguistic symbols.

There is no way for the political scientist to escape the

tyranny of words. Political life is saturated with verbalism; symbols can come to serve as substitutes for the reality to which they once referred but which may no longer exist. Political institutions are the outgrowth of communicated experience that has been discussed, debated, and finally verbalized in a distinctive form. Defining political phenomena is always a difficult problem. If political science concepts are to have any stable meaning, they must have clear referents in the real world of observable empirical data. No matter how abstract our concepts may become, they must be relevant and empirically operational if they are going to be meaningful in the realm of academic discourse.

Professor Murray Edelman points out that "there is nothing about any symbol that requires that it stand for only one thing."[6] The meanings are not in the symbols; they are in society and in men. Our language is embedded in culture; the linguistic symbols men use structure their perceptions and experiences. Our shorthand symbols point to a whole complex of processes and relationships among things. Despite all of the difficulties associated with symbolic communication, political analysis cannot proceed without the necessary tools to permit abstraction and generalization about different aspects of concrete reality. A major task for students is the mastery of a technical vocabulary and a conceptual understanding which allows them to explore complex political phenomena with sophistication and skill.

[6] Murray Edelman, *The Symbolic Uses of Politics* (Urbana: University of Illinois Press, 1964), p. 11.

TWO

Approaches to the Study of Comparative Politics

Approaches are tools by which we arrive at greater political understanding. In the light of the previous discussion, it will not surprise the student to find that a diversity of approaches are used by political scientists to attack the complexity of political systems and behavior. In order to discuss what approaches should be used, it is obviously necessary to have an idea of what is to be studied. The fact that the subject matter is in a state of flux confronts the student of comparative politics with many difficult problems and hard choices.

The study of comparative politics operates upon a much broader base than it did two decades ago. It is necessary to examine an infinitely more varied nexus of forces than was the case in an earlier generation. While the range and vitality of new approaches is a sign of health in the discipline, these make it impractical to attempt to identify each possible line of approach separately. We can present the most important current approaches in order to give the student a bird's-eye view of the rich methodological terrain confronting him. This is an age of reexamination of concepts, approaches, theories, and models of analysis. We are required to choose our conceptual frameworks and approaches with great care, for they decide the contours of any investigation and may determine the value of the outcome. Of course, approaches are by no means mutually exclusive and one may employ two or more approaches in analyzing the same problem. Such eclecticism is probably as desirable as it is necessary.

Because differences exist regarding what is significant for purposes of comparison, approaches contain criteria for selecting problems and relevant data for intensive analysis. One can, indeed, find works in political science which make little or no attempt to select and order their data. Such books simply collect and classify information. No explanations are offered, no conceptual scheme is advanced, and no conclusions are reached. While it is necessary to have a reservoir of facts available for scholarship, the good scholar does not simply assemble facts in the expectation that the process will somehow lead to significant knowledge. The scholar deals with relationships among facts rather than with series of isolated facts. Moreover, the facts of political science are by no means foreordained; they are selected by political scientists. New approaches draw new facts into the field by acting as magnets for previously overlooked data.

We can readily see, then, that there are alternative ways of thinking about facts and ordering them in the search for knowledge. That is why it has been asserted that "it is an utterly superficial view . . . that the truth is to be found by 'studying the facts.' "[1] The facts are varied and infinite; they must be rendered meaningful. Approaches aid in defining the kinds of facts which are relevant. Without delimiting the range of factual data to be considered, we would be embarked on an aimless, endless quest; we simply must think in terms of classes, categories, and types rather than in terms of the multitude of separate facts involved. The following approaches are those in use among students of comparative politics. Others might have been included, but for the most part these are either of minor importance or fall within one of the general approaches discussed.

---

[1] Morris R. Cohen and Ernest Nagel, *An Introduction to Logic and Scientific Method* (New York: Harcourt, Brace, 1934), p. 199.

Legal-Institutional Approaches

One of the oldest methods of analyzing politics is the legal-institutional approach. It is probably the most familiar approach to most readers of this book who have completed a course in American government. In fact, the classic example of the legal-institutional approach to political science data is found in the volume *Introduction to American Government,* by Frederick Ogg and P. Orman Ray. In the field of European government and politics, the approach is seen in *Major Foreign Powers,* by Gwendolen M. Carter and John H. Herz.

A great deal of scholarly effort has been devoted to the study of political institutions. For example, there have been many comparative studies of cabinets, electoral systems, legislative bodies, executives, courts, political parties, bureaucracies, and the like. Roughly the same kinds of institutions can be found in most political systems (especially in the Western world), and this permits the scholar to immerse himself in a vast sea of empirical data.

Institutional comparison involves a relatively detailed description of the institution under analysis followed by an attempt to clarify which details are similar or different. There are several ways of comparing political institutions. We can compare the institutions of a particular political system with each other at a given time. Most of the introductory courses in American national government are taught in this way. Congress is compared with the Presidency and the Supreme Court. The Articles of Confederation are compared with the document drafted at Philadelphia in 1787. Political parties and interest groups may be studied comparatively. Different aspects of these institutions can also be compared. Thus we may compare the internal structure of the House of Representatives to that of the Senate, examining the different functions they perform, their patterns of decision-making and leadership, and their share of power in the political system.

Painting on a broader canvas, we can compare the political institutions of one country with those of another, comparing them as sets or even systems of institutions. The political order consists of those institutions within which men acquire, wield, or influence the distribution of power and authority within the structures of society. Distinctive political institutions have emerged in many different historical contexts and for a variety of reasons. At times, new problems that required organized action by society as a whole were the stimuli which led to the creation of appropriate institutions to cope with the problems. Political institutions are social instruments for the attainment of certain kinds of community goals.[2]

The differentiated political institutions that make up the state are not often found in primitive societies. However, in the so-called advanced societies, there are many institutions which can be analyzed by using various comparative criteria. Institutions are the hallmark of Western civilization, for Western man has been an institution-building animal. We see this process exemplified when we look at the evolution of democratic institutions over hundreds of years in Great Britain.

Political and social institutions in a system tend to be interrelated. The institution of government is very broad and subsumes many different elements. The institutions of a society offer a framework of meanings and values to guide individuals as they make decisions in all aspects of their lives. Each institution contains many values within itself; every institution centers around fundamental human needs, permanently uniting a group of people in some cooperative endeavor. One of the major ways in which political systems differ from one another lies in the amount of power each grants to specific types of institutions. One system may have a powerful legislature; another may have a weak legislature and a strong executive; a third may be dominated by the political resources of the military.

Why should a particular political institution in a given system be powerful in one country and weak in another? The relative power of institutions within various political systems is

---

2 Roy C. Macridis, *The Study of Comparative Government* (New York: Doubleday and Company, 1955), p. 56.

the subject of much of the literature of comparative politics. Each political and social institution has resources and handicaps in the struggle for political power. Legislatures, for example, have become powerful by becoming the centers of political information. Executives tend to be both skilled in the utilization of resources and motivated to use them at a high level, in addition to possessing a monopoly of political violence. Courts may play a powerful role in government by their prestige and aura of legitimacy, which combine to give them a powerful role in affairs of state. We study institutions because they provide the means whereby a number of people can act collectively on the basis of common understandings. Of course, those meanings and values which constitute an institution do not exist in themselves but are observed in the regularity and the consistency of human behavior.

Reference to consistency of behavior does not imply, however, that every person who is a member of an institution is expected to manifest the same behavior. Each institution has a division of labor among its participants. There are numerous roles involved in the operation of an institution, and each role complements others to make the institution operate. Some of these roles are especially important in the operation of the institution and are filled by a small number of the group members. In any large organization the enforcement of rules and regulations is formally accomplished by the officers of the organization, who are given authority over the behavior of other members. The complex of institutions that constitute the organization of political authority is referred to as the *state*. This is an inclusive concept that covers all aspects of policy making and enforcement of legal sanctions. Since the concept is so inclusive, we frequently find more utility in the concept of *government*, a term which expresses the concrete institutional organization through which the most important political functions are performed. Government is simply the agency through which the state acts in the political community. A government is to a state what a board of directors is to a corporation.

Human societies are structured; they resemble a building

rather than a pile of stones, and the architecture of the building is determined by its institutions. A society with many and complicated institutions has a cohesiveness which guides behavior patterns and stabilizes the total culture in an enduring manner. Institutions provide ready-made forms of social relations and social roles for the individual. They simplify social behavior for the individual by creating expectations which are prearranged for the person before he enters the society. Ways of thinking and behaving that are institutionalized "make sense" to people. Institutions contain the systematic expectations of a society and are a source of security for the great majority of people in their day-to-day activities. We shall see that there are certain patterns within political institutions that appear to be characteristic of particular cultures.

A political system is an operational whole which enables a group of human beings to arrive at decisions and to evolve policies, by way of institutions, which provide them with the means of effective cooperation. A political institution is any persistent system of activities and expectations having a function in the political system. These activities are regularized or expected or authorized, and they are more or less persistent. Government is the most comprehensive political institution.

All institutions are subject to continuous change. The activity that goes on in a political system is constantly altering political institutions, although the facade may remain the same. Some of the changes are a result of the maturing process which all institutions naturally undergo. Other changes are caused by outside factors. Change occurs most dramatically under conditions of crisis, but not all crises necessarily stimulate alterations. Nevertheless, periods of crisis can be crucial in creating changes, whether temporary or permanent. The institutional framework that fits a period of full employment and prosperity may falter during a time of economic recession. The structure appropriate to a time of peace may have to be streamlined to meet the exigencies of war. When revolutions occur, there is generally an overhauling of the institutions of the political system. However, political institutions often exhibit an inertia which results in their survival from one political system into another.

In many cases, institutions which are carried over are changed in their nature, because their function and purpose are altered. Regardless of how they occur such institutional changes are always worthy of intensive research by political scientists. Institutions may maintain their names and outward appearance while undergoing radical internal changes through actions and events. New institutions and new concepts of legality may replace the old ones. As a generalization, one can state that institutional change is relatively slow because the components of institutions tend to hang together and reinforce each other.

Institutions vary in the degree of control they have over the lives of their members. The role played by governmental institutions looms very large indeed in all modern, technologically advanced societies. Government cannot be escaped; it is without doubt the most powerful single instrument of social control in modern society. Government is a phenomenon that is integral with the social life of man and seemingly inherent in the very nature of social order. It takes different institutional forms according to the interplay of social forces in each society. Groups are distinguished from each other by their institutions; societies differ in the total system formed by their institutions. The arrangement and disposition of institutional structures within a society is what gives it a special character. It is instructional to examine diverse forms of institutional arrangements, since they are decisive in channeling the processes of social change. Some political systems have flexible institutional structures; other systems are marked by rigid institutional structures which retard innovation and change.

In making comparisons at the institutional level, we must take various characteristics into account. The following aspects are worthy of consideration: the genesis of the institution, the purpose of its creation, the process of growth of the institution, the means by which the institution is perpetuated, the manner in which new members are brought into the institution, the external and internal structures of the institution, the relationship of the institution to other institutions and to the general community, the spheres of life in which the institution operates, the functions of the institution, and the importance of the institution in the total political and social configuration of the system being examined. Institutional analysis of this kind is neither simple nor obvious but requires intellectual skills of a high order of precision and sophistication. Political institutions are the outcome of the interaction of many complex phenomena involving different levels of abstraction. There are various explanations and interpretations put forth by political scientists in their analysis of concrete institutional phenomena. In fact, the meaning of an institutional approach varies with the definition of *institution* adopted by the investigator. Some students conceive of institutions in a much narrower sense than others. The danger of such circumscribed conceptions is that they may lead to a mere accumulation of isolated bits of information.

It is precisely this tendency to miss the forest for the trees that has led to discrediting of the institutional approach in the minds of many political scientists. The traditional focus of the political scientist's interest, whether broadly or narrowly conceived, has been the formal institutions of government. The primary emphasis has been on the descriptive study of national institutions, constitutional structures, and administrative organizations. The field of vision was restricted to empirical investigation of the formal, legal, institutional aspects of governmental systems.

It should come as no great surprise that the detailed examination of the institutional ramifications of government was characteristic of the early efforts of political scientists. After all, each of the social science disciplines is partly based on the definition of a certain number of institutions. Each discipline employs standardized analytic procedures to examine the technical institutional arrangements which fall within its scope. In the case of political science, the approach had utility because it both permitted the study of easily observable and recordable phenomena and precluded the use of subjectively derived data. There was a natural desire to give the young discipline a definite and concrete framework vis-à-vis the established, older social sciences, which were also striving for scientific reliability.

Because political behavior invariably occurs in institutional settings, the student of comparative politics cannot afford to ignore these primary units of analysis. A great deal of political behavior can be accounted for by viewing it as a result of institutional factors within the political structure. Institutions are the apparatus through which the power process functions in society organized as a state. It is not the institutional approach, *per se*, which leads to the mere gathering and filing of formal, empirical political data. Rather, it is the too-narrow application of that approach which has led to its rejection by many political scientists.

Even used wisely, however, the institutional approach must be supplemented by other tools and concepts if it is to attain its full explanatory power. A purely architectural appreciation of political institutions yields little or no insight into the dynamics of political behavior. The study of the formal framework of institutions may be quite misleading as to their vitality or real importance in the political system. The institutional school of analysis too often made the error of considering institutions comparable simply because they happened to bear the same label when it is quite obvious that institutions of government which bear the same name can be utterly different in their actual functioning. The comparison of such external aspects, without regard to the environment within which they operate and the different functions they perform, may actually be worse than useless.

Another frequent error of institutional analysis is the failure to recognize that institutions cannot exist physically apart from the persons who operate them. In our previous discussion of concepts, we noted the dangers of reification. Some of the institutionalists have been guilty of this usage in their analysis of courts, legislatures, and bureaucracies. Some metaphorical language is, perhaps, unavoidable but we must never forget that any collectivities exist and behave only to the extent the people composing them act in certain ways. Institutions are men and women acting under a particular discipline. Thus we can speak of a legislature as an institution in that the legislators are charged with the performance of certain functions in a regularized and persistent way. Most people whose behavior they are called on to guide will conform to their decisions as authoritative.

This does not imply that the legislature is not a real, meaningful unit with structural properties and functions of its own but, rather, that as a collectivity it derives its basic meaning from the actions of human beings who compose and act through it. It is, therefore, an integrated system of behavior operating in an institutional setting. The relationship between institution and behavior is complementary. Institutional arrangements reflect behavioral patterns that have been stabilized through the passage of time. The institutional environment cannot be ignored by the student of comparative politics.

If we bear in mind that institutions operate for and through people and that they grow and change through actual human behavior, we shall avoid static conceptualization in our approach to institutions. We shall free ourselves from narrowly descriptive frames of reference which are confining and unproductive. Our concern will turn away from a formal, legalistic approach to a consideration of political dynamics and the deeper meaning of the political process. As a result, our comparisons will attain greater depth and reliability. We will be able to cope with the fact that an institution can change its functions and that the same function can be performed by several institutions. Institutions are not correlated simply and directly to their functions; typically, institutions are multifunctional and overlap each other in a network of interdependence. Each institution influences all the others in varying degrees and in turn is influenced by them. That is why a narrow, formalistic approach to such an enormous complexity is bound to be highly inadequate.

We have considered, in a general manner, the characteristic elements associated with institutional approaches to political data. The limitations discussed in the above presentation should not lead the student to reject the approach out of hand. Institutional analysis, if done well, can endure over the years. The works of Carl J. Friedrich and Herman Finer, though written a generation ago, are still worth the careful attention of the student beginning the study of comparative government and politics.[3] The best work of the institutionalists sought to find, through empirical comparisons, the key practices, institutions, and factors that were the crucial derivatives of governmental power. By using the art of comparison, sometimes in an intuitive, speculative fashion, they attempted to discover the general in the particular. Instead of dismissing their efforts in a cavalier manner, we should recognize that it was through their efforts that the early inheritance of comparative politics has been transmitted to us. Today, institutional approaches can be fruitfully blended with other approaches to provide a rounded analysis of political phenomena.

Approaches Focusing on Decision-Making

The foregoing presentation of salient characteristics of the institutional approach leads us to another major conceptual scheme for political analysis, that of decision-making. Decision-making and the process of deliberation are manifested through institutional political structures. Students who employ this approach conceive of a political system as primarily a mechanism for the making of decisions. Decision-making is perceived as the most pervasive function of politics. It can be discovered in any political system from the most primitive, traditional systems to the most complex, modernized ones. The universality of the decision-making function permits the most wide ranging comparisons of highly dissimilar systems.

Perhaps the best known scholar in the area of decision-

---

[3] See Carl J. Friedrich, *Constitutional Government and Democracy* (Boston: Ginn, 1941), and Herman Finer, *The Theory and Practice of Modern Government* (New York: Holt, Rinehart and Winston, 1949).

making analysis is Richard C. Snyder. Although Professor Snyder's own research is devoted mainly to the application of decision-making methodology in the field of international politics, he has also argued that a decision-making frame of reference can be profitably used in the study of all political phenomena.[4] Among the first of the specialists in comparative politics to incorporate the concept of decision-making within the boundaries of an analytic scheme was Ray C. Macridis.[5] Current social science literature reflects an increased concern with the analysis of political, social, and economic decision-making.

Decision-making denotes the dynamic process of interaction among all participants, official as well as nonofficial, who determine a particular public policy choice. Decision-making studies focus on all the factors relevant to a policy choice and not just on the formal legal relationships of decision makers. In describing the decision process of any political system we expect to find that several official and unofficial participants in the political arena are implicated at any given time in the political process. Many political actors are located outside the authoritative machinery of the community.[6] It would seem vital to distinguish between the official actors who seem to decide and the unofficial actors who operate publicly or behind the scenes. Conceived in such broad terms, decision-making analysis can illuminate the activities of pressure groups in political life.

A basic part of behavior in political and social institutions is the making of decisions. All members of such structures are constantly choosing one course of action over other possible ones. They are choosing among ends and means. All important

---

4 See Richard C. Snyder, "A Decision-Making Approach to the Study of Political Phenomena," in Roland Young, editor, *Approaches to the Study of Politics* (Evanston, Ill.: Northwestern University Press, 1958), pp. 3-38.

5 Macridis, *Study of Comparative Government*, pp. 37-44.

6 Professor Snyder's scheme assumes that only those who are government officials are to be viewed as decision makers. For his justification of this posture, see Snyder, *"A Decision-Making Approach,"* pp. 15-16.

decisions are made up of a group of lesser decisions and are themselves part of a group of larger decisions. Decision makers respond in one way rather than another to each situation which confronts them. All decisions are judgments about alternatives. We should always keep in mind that the alternative of nonaction is just as real as any of the available action alternatives.

If one chooses a decision-making approach to comparative political data, the following categories of analysis are suggestive of the research design:

1. *Identification of the Decision Makers*

The approach focuses inquiry on a class of actors called decision makers. In every system we shall find persons or institutions through which authoritative decisions are made. One index of where power resides in a society is the social composition of those who hold official positions and make political decisions. The social background of decision makers, for example, often offers important clues to their values and behavior. In all political systems, only a small number of persons actually exercise power and authority.

The question of who makes the decisions cannot be answered by an examination of the formal legal structure alone. Very frequently we must look behind the formal facade to locate the real locus of the decision-making power. Regardless of their location in the system, the decision makers respond to stimuli, value certain objectives, make evaluations of alternative courses of action, and allocate resources to various endeavors.

The characteristics of decision makers can be studied from many perspectives such as biographical data, attitude studies, aspects of personality, psychological motivation, and the like. All of these aspects can be subjected to systematic empirical investigation.

2. *Forms of Selection of Decision Makers*

Every political system has its own method of selecting political leaders. The manner of selection differs from one system to another. A powerful electorate can place its men in office and transmit its preferences through the control of government decision-making machinery. In some societies, the electorate may be based on a narrow segment of the polity whose decisions are not respected by other groups in the society. Among the strongest national electorates in the world today are the voters of Great Britain. They possess a significant share of power in their political system. The voters of Switzerland are, perhaps, even stronger, because they are called upon to decide many matters directly through referenda.

Societies differ in the relative importance they assign to the ascriptive and achievement criteria of status. Ascription of status means that a society applies certain criteria of evaluation to the individual without any action being taken on his part. These criteria used include factors such as race, religion, ancestry, education, power, occupation and wealth. The traditional Indian caste system was based almost entirely upon ascription.

Achievement criteria, on the other hand, depend upon demonstrations of individual effort and capacity which can be evaluated by society on their respective merits. There is considerable variation from society to society in the significance attached to these highly differing criteria. Many times they have important political consequences which should not be neglected by the analyst. Frequently, the criteria are built into the institutions of the political system. After all, there is only one way to become a candidate for monarch of Great Britain and that is to be born in Buckingham Palace with the proper genes.

3. *The Institutional Setting for Decision-Making*

It seems obvious that the institutional approach can be comfortably linked with a decision-making approach. The decision makers carry on their activities in a setting with internal and external aspects. We must search for the factors and conditions relevant to the behavior of decision makers, both within the organization and outside of its confines. Once we have identified the various institutional units, we can assess their role in the decision-making process of a given political system.

The setting changes constantly as social and economic

groups press their claims upon the government. Political leadership sifts these claims and articulates them in the form of decisions. Conflicting claims and demands are translated into accepted decisions. Every group of decision makers functions in a larger setting. There are boundaries which encompass the actors and activities to be observed and explained. Political relationships must be treated in the light of the interplay of forces that constitute the dynamics of politics.

There are two aspects of the setting which deserve analysis, the social setting and the political, institutional setting. An adequate concept of decision-making will include in the social setting such categories as public opinion, ideological orientations, group structures and functions, and major institutional patterns of the society. Every action taken by decision makers has consequences in the society at large. The political, institutional setting consists of the vast complex of rules and organizations which make up the constituent elements of government. Since any decisional unit is likely to exist simultaneously with other units, the reciprocal impact of courses of action adopted must be analyzed. Each unit is an organization in itself, and each unit is a component of the total policy-making structure.[7]

In modern Western states, the decision-making process is carried on by a bureaucratic elite. Division of labor and specialization are highly developed. Organization implies highly formalized relationships among the members of the decision-making units. These patterns of decision-making can be subjected to analysis. The kinds of action taken by a set of decision makers will be a function of the major institutional patterns and social values of their society.

4. *The Process of Decision-Making*

The following definition of decision-making is put forth by Richard Snyder. "Decision-making results in the selection from a socially defined, limited number of problematical, al-

---

[7] For an interesting application of decision-making analysis to a political institution, see Edgar S. Furniss, Jr., *The Office of Premier in French Foreign Policy-making* (Princeton, N.J.: Foreign Policy Analysis Project, 1954).

ternative projects (*i.e.,* courses of action) of one project to bring about the particular future state of affairs envisaged by the decision makers."[8] Decision-making is a process: a decision is not an isolated act but is the climax of a whole set of interrelated acts which supplement each other. *Selection* indicates deliberation and calculation. In every system there are procedures through which decisions are arrived at and articulated. For decision-making to take place, certain persons must be empowered to act under certain conditions. There is a formal structure of decision-making based on the allocation of power and responsibility.

Decision-making is a sequence of activities. Viewed as a rational process, decisions have many dimensions and almost infinitely complex interrelations. *Process* refers to the sum of the particular techniques, methods, and procedures by which a given decision is made. It is the *how* of decision-making as distinct from *who* decides. Any decision can be made in a number of different ways. There are social processes which are involved in the making of a given political decision, complemented by intellectual and cultural processes which give to each society a distinctive mode of decision-making. Each decision maker is a product of the national culture; cultural values shape political decisions in many subtle ways.

The process of discussion and examination of a problem is at the heart of the deliberative process. There are rational techniques for the identification of a problem in modern, advanced societies. The clarification of problems takes various forms. In a democracy, the problems are debated through channels of communication. The schools and the mass media attempt to put the various problems in perspective. Decisions have tended to become increasingly complex and technical in content. Every political problem involves an infinite number of variables: decision makers can deal with only a tiny fraction of what is possibly relevant, even with the help of electronic computers. We can never know all the consequences of any act or

---

[8] Snyder, "A Decision-Making Approach," p. 19.

decision. Most decisions, political or other, are made with extremely limited knowledge of their alternative costs and values.

A decision can reflect only the information possessed at the time the decision is made. Knowledge is required, and knowledge rests upon adequate information of many sorts. One of the principal political resources is politically useful information and ideas. An important kind of political information consists of ideas about what may be done to cope with problems. A bureaucracy accumulates considerable stores of information; in many systems bureaucrats are expected to take the lead in preparing and proposing new ideas and programs. This makes bureaucrats a major source of policy innovation. In other systems, the bureaucracy may have a counterproductive influence on decision-making by suppressing information, thereby causing stagnation rather than change. Regardless of its influence for better or worse, the bureaucracy is the only political institution which is necessarily specialized and composed of experts. The power position of a fully developed bureaucracy is always imposing in its potential for influencing the decision-making process.

Of course, information alone is not enough; the decision maker must have the capacity to organize and interpret the data and to estimate the effects of policy alternatives. He must attempt to know all the possible choices in a situation. He must think in terms of probable consequences. Finally, he must have a scale of values that will permit him to evaluate the sets of consequences involved in his choice. There are pools of information available to the decision maker in the social setting and the institutional setting. The distribution of this information may have a significant effect on images decision makers have of a particular problem. One of the most difficult problems involved in the functioning of a political system is to make the necessary information available to the right people at the right time. There are all kinds of barriers to effective communication which must be overcome in the decision-making process.

The relationship between communication and political action has only recently been explored by political scientists.

Politics and communications are intertwined *within* any organization, since its systems of power and decision-making affect and are affected by the communications network through which the rules and norms of the organization are circulated. In any system, information is stored, whether in filing cabinets or in the brains of political personnel. By way of metaphor, we can say that an organization has a memory which permits selection and rejection of various options on the basis of past experiences. Skills and resources must be brought to bear at strategic points in the decision-making process. "Communicatory activity is considered political by virtue of the consequences, actual and potential, that it has for the functioning of the political system."[9]

5. *The Implementation of Decisions*

A political decision is a complex thing. The complexity lies not only in the decision-making process but in the details of implementing a decision once it has been selected. There is likely to be a substantial amount of intellectual conflict in the reaching of any decision. The occasion for a decision arises when a change occurs in a situation, with the result that a condition once deemed satisfactory is now regarded as unsatisfactory. A decision is the selection of a response to cope with such an altered situation.

The implementation of a decision also represents a process whereby general policy objectives become more specific and concrete. During this separate process of implementation, original aims may be distorted, reinterpreted, or otherwise altered. A lethargic bureaucracy may lack the vitality and imagination to implement a decision made by officials in the higher echelons of the power structure. Political life falls into hierarchies of sets and subsets of decisions and rarely presents isolated decisions. One faces a set of alternatives: to go to war or not to go to war; to nationalize the steel industry or not to nationalize; to form a coalition cabinet or try to govern in a different fashion—the list of alternatives is virtually endless.

---

[9] For an introduction to the subject of communication (with special reference to comparative politics), see Richard R. Fagen, *Politics and Communication* (Boston: Little, Brown, 1966).

Within the various alternatives lies a series of subsets of decisions; each subset entails subordinate subsets. A major problem in formulating any decision is to determine which set or sets are open for decision and which are *given* or closed. Complicated decisions require judgments about decision techniques and about the formulation of the question.

6. *Evaluation of the Content of Decisions*

A final intellectual task which the student of decision-making may attempt is evaluating the decisions which are made. No political analysis has ever been undertaken without touching values. Normative statements express conceptions of the desirable; most decisions involve value preferences on the part of the decision makers, in the sense that they endorse certain ends, purposes, or norms. The latter can be evaluated by establishing criteria of performance, whether conceived in terms of morality, efficiency, rationality, justice, or the like.

At times, judgments relative to the content of decisions will be expressed in terms of the relative importance or urgency of the decisions. Whether there can, indeed, be a preordained ranking of the basic objectives of a political community has occupied the attention of political philosophers. Regardless of one's answer to this question, the value orientation of a community is always a necessary element in the evaluation of decisions made by the political agents of the community.

Value judgments and existential judgments are interrelated, and all of political life is shaped by the interaction of the two types of data. The experiencing of values is as much a primary human experience as the observation of facts. Some values may be experienced only by some persons, but the basic values are experienced by most persons. Although there is disagreement in political science about values as objects of inquiry and about their legitimate place in research, the meaning and ethical evaluations people attribute to social behavior cannot be ignored.[10] A basic premise of the normative approach in

---

[10] For an extended discussion of this question, see Charles S. Hyneman, *The Study of Politics* (Urbana: University of Illinois Press, 1959), pp. 174-92.

comparative politics is that the analyst cannot perceive the meaning of values to others until he identifies the significance of these values to himself.

Frequently decision makers do not define clearly the values that their actions reflect. In certain cases, they may even be unaware of some of the values implicit in their behavior; they may also be ignorant of the values held by those for whom they are making the decisions. At times, decisions may be made without full consideration being given to questions about values. In particular, decision makers may overlook the fact that some values must often be purchased at some cost to other things which are valued. Decision makers operate within a regime of competing values. Particular values rise to or fall from ascendancy over others. This being so, continuing evaluation of the content of decisions would appear to be a necessary intellectual task for the student who adopts a decision-making approach to political data.

The Power Approach

Power is one of the oldest and most widely used concepts in the study of political phenomena. References to power are found throughout the vast literature on the history of political thought. The classic texts of ancient Chinese, Greek, Roman, Indian, and Egyptian civilizations discuss the varieties, uses, and justifications of power. In *The Prince,* Niccolo Machiavelli presented the principle that the purpose of politics is to increase political power. Machiavelli devotes several chapters of *The Prince* to a detailed description of the moral qualities a ruler must have and the role of these in the maintenance of his power. For Machiavelli, political science becomes a technique for the successful manipulation of power; political success is measured by the extent to which this is achieved. Because of his emphasis on power and his secular point of view, Machiavelli is often called the first modern political theorist. Certainly he did cast political philosophy in a new light by his insistence that techniques of effective statecraft must be rooted in the realities of human nature and social power, but Machiavelli would hardly qualify as a political scientist in the modern sense. His writings consist of completely unsystematic reflection combined with shrewd admonitions to the ruler. Nevertheless, he saw clearly that rule is institutionalized political power and that a stable government derives from the fact that power imposes a conformity of conduct which becomes habitual with the citizenry.

In contemporary political science, the concept of power occupies a position of major importance. Some analysts maintain that the concept is central to all political inquiry. Professor Hans J. Morgenthau opens his textbook *Politics among Nations* with this statement of intellectual conviction: "International politics, like all politics, is a struggle for power." One might note in this regard that the power approach, like that of decision-making, was designed primarily for the study of international politics. Proponents of both approaches argue that either can be applied to all study of political phenomena. Advocates of the power approach maintain that the struggle for power is universal and both domestic and international politics are characterized by this struggle. The struggle is the same; only the stages on which it takes place are different.

The longevity of the power approach suggests that many political scientists have felt it does illuminate political behavior. Thus we find two analysts noted for their empirical rigor asserting: "The concept of power is perhaps the most fundamental in the whole of political science; the political process is the shaping, distribution, and exercise of power."[11] One of the earliest statements endorsing power as a central orienting concept for political data was Professor George E. G. Catlin in his *Science and Method of Politics.* Catlin contends that the struggle of wills is the foundation of politics and the core around which causal political theory can be constructed. In other words, the distinctly political act is the desire to execute one's desires. All people seek to assert themselves; this act of the will is a political fact of life which appears constantly in all

---

[11] Harold D. Lasswell and Abraham Kaplan, *Power and Society: A Framework for Political Inquiry* (New Haven, Conn.: Yale University Press, 1950), p. 75.

human activity. This is a prime psychological fact upon which a science of politics can be constructed. Man, the political animal, seeks power as man, the economic animal, seeks wealth. The essence of the struggle for power, in Catlin's view, involves control over the will of others.

A second student of power phenomena is Harold D. Lasswell, who has consistently maintained that the major concepts guiding political research must be power and values. Professor Lasswell argues that the polity is an arena in which the contestants strive to accomplish their purposes by influencing outcomes and effects. Political analysis becomes the study of changes in the shape and composition of the value pattern of society. More specifically, according to Lasswell, political science research must focus on influence and the influential, and he titled one of his best-known books *Politics: Who Gets What, When, How.* In this volume, Lasswell explores the sources of power held by a political elite. He analyzes the means used by elites to arrive at and survive in the seat of power. Those who followed in the path outlined by Lasswell concentrated on the characteristics of governing groups, including aspects such as class origin, personality traits, and the instruments employed to attain positions of power and influence.

Lasswell is cognizant of the tendency in mass societies for power to concentrate in the hands of a minority. He therefore advocates a study of the power of the elite as most promising for research orientations. Political science becomes the science of governors and leaders: it examines their origin, structure, prerogatives, and the scope and foundations of the obedience given to them. Political power, of course, will be manifested within the total social power configuration of a particular system. The quest for power is usually justified in terms of larger schemes of values. Power, in order to be respected, must be wrapped in garments which serve the aspirations and the recognized cultural values of society.[12] An adequate knowledge of power relations involves an understanding of the grounds on

---

[12] Hans Gerth and C. Wright Mills, *Character and Social Structure* (New York: Harcourt, Brace and World, 1953), p. 324.

which a power holder claims obedience, and the terms on which the follower feels an obligation to obey. Here we shall encounter such aspects as manipulation of the symbols of justification and legitimation of the authority of the power holder. Political figures who ignore the common values of their following do so at considerable peril. That is why Lasswell, in his later work, began to explore the total configuration of power in relation to values and the effect of values on public policy.

A political sociologist, Robert M. MacIver, has written on the concept of power with great insight. In particular, MacIver has demonstrated the fallacy of equating power with authority. Power itself is not authority, although many writers fail to make the necessary distinction. Power alone has no legitimacy, no mandate, but authority is the established right, within the social order, to determine policies and settle controversies. The accent is primarily on right, not power. Even the most ruthless dictator will attempt to clothe himself with authority and legitimacy. Authority is fundamental if the social order is to be sustained. Political power has a mission and an authority to which no other element of society can lay claim, for it alone is the organ of the whole community. Under all conditions, political power is the final regulatory control of the social order.

Power, then, may be the catalyst by which political leaders can secure compliance. Power can be the lubricant of the body politic, but power is a relationship among men, not a characteristic or a quality possessed by them. As Professor MacIver explains:

> Social power is in the last resort derivative, not inherent in the groups or individuals who direct, control, or coerce other groups or individuals. The power a man has is the power he disposes; it is not intrinsically his own. He cannot command unless another obeys. He cannot control unless the social organization invests him with the apparatus of control. We are prone to confuse power with the means, agencies, or instruments of power. But power resides in the social disposition of these means, depends on the rights and obligations developed in a society.[13]

---

[13] Robert M. MacIver, *The Web of Government* (New York: MacMillan, 1951), pp. 107-108.

MacIver makes the important point that political leadership is more often than not associated with office holding, which provides an increment of legal power to the incumbent and which in turn contributes to acceptance of that leadership by members of society. The particular *style* of leadership employed to achieve loyalty from a following will depend upon a great many political, social, and economic factors relative to the existing situation. Each leader will attempt to identify with various clusters of values to secure a following; he will have to be sensitive to the norms and needs of his following if he is to maintain his position of power and authority.

However defined, power is a relational concept which implies the interaction of two or more persons or groups of persons. Because of the number of different contexts in which the term is used, no definition of power has gained general acceptance among political scientists. In the interests of conceptual clarity, several different types of power should be distinguished. For any concept to have analytical utility, it is necessary that the meaning of the concept be defined as precisely as possible. Professor Robert Dahl has written one of the clearest statements of the dimensions of power as an analytical tool.[14]

Although there have been several different definitions of power offered by political scientists, most of them incorporate various aspects of the omnipresent social relationships of command and obedience. Power, as we have seen, is transformed into authority through the use of the appropriate political values and institutions. Political power is surrounded by other elements of social power and is exercised within the totality of the social power configuration of a given system. The division of society into power holders and subjects is practically a universal phenomenon; however, the exercise of power is conditioned by cultural elements which are of crucial importance to political analysis. The great importance of economic factors for political

---

[14] Robert A. Dahl, "The Concept of Power," *Behavioral Science,* July 1957, pp. 201-15.

power is another relevant consideration. Studies in the psychology of the individual and of groups have also become more important in recent research on power relationships. Power relationships cannot be evaluated as if they were indivisible: each facet of a relationship has a separable power division. Power is unevenly distributed in society. Power is situational, relative, and multifaceted. It is one thing to define power and quite another to observe its effects.

Political power is an elusive concept. Nevertheless, since no society in recorded history has ever been able to dispense with political power, the problems revolving around its use and abuse continue to pose questions of major significance for the attention of the political scientist. The balance and allocation of power presents one of the greatest of political problems: the balance between regions, interests, functions, and authorities. The concentration and diffusion of power and responsibility are a central problem within any political system, regardless of its ideological structure.

The face of power is reflected most vividly in its distribution in various social settings. A systematic theory of the process of power in politics would require empirical data on the characteristics of various types of decision makers, as well as an investigation of their function within a variety of cultural contexts. Such theory would involve the careful analysis of the formal and informal structures of those groups which seek access to political power. The interlocking functions of the agents and of the techniques of political power must be examined to explain the character and determinants of political consensus.

Power and decision-making approaches are distinctly complementary. For decision-making to take place, certain persons must be given the power to act and must act under certain conditions. Responsibilities must be assigned and orders must be obeyed. The allocation of power and responsibility prevails among decision-making units as well as within them. The evidence of the formal allocation of power in a political system can be discovered by examining the institutional arrangements. Informal or indirect influences upon political authority must also be carefully evaluated. Generally speaking, political power is exercised by the state and its organs to achieve certain commonly shared objectives of the society.

The way in which an organization is structured has an important bearing on the distribution of power within it. For example, there are hierarchical types of organizations that place severe limits on the initiative of their members. Some organizations, such as the military, are hierarchically constructed because their objectives and functions require it. The model of power distribution in such an organization is symbolized by a pyramid, with power concentrated at the top and orders passed down the line requiring precise obedience in accordance with rigidly prescribed routines.

Other organizations are characterized by more flexible procedures, with more willingness to tolerate dissent. The process of democratization operating in the twentieth century has provided for greater popular participation and control in many organizations. The broad distinction between authoritarian and flexible types of organization is seen in the contrast between dictatorial and democratic governments. Even in an autocratic regime, however, the people are continually judging their leaders, and these evaluations act as a popular constraint upon the rulers.

There is, then, a long tradition in political science of using power as an organizing concept for the collection and analysis of political data. William A. Robson summarizes this concern when he states, "It is with power in society that political science is primarily concerned—its nature, basis, processes, scope and results. The focus of interest . . . centers on the struggle to gain or retain power, to exercise power or influence over others, or to resist that exercise."[15] Politics, when considered as a struggle for power, centers around who shall determine public policy and what that policy shall be. Both the locus and exercise of power are affected by the specific political institutions which

---

[15] William A. Robson, *The University Teaching of Social Sciences: Political Science* (Paris: United Nations Educational, Scientific, and Cultural Organization, 1954), pp. 17-18.

determine how public officials are chosen and which define the limits of their power and the procedures they are required to follow.

The complicated relations between social structure and political power are manifested in each political system under investigation. The struggle for power in any given society, whether democratic or totalitarian, involves conflict not merely among individuals and political parties but also among social groups that seek to promote or secure their interests. Comparative analysis can be pursued by isolating such groups and comparing their relationships to the political organs of the respective systems. The impact of such groups upon political activity can be studied in terms of several key variables.

Power has been a key concept in the tradition of Western political thought because the power of man over man has existed from the dawn of society. All the manifestations of power that operate in human society are set in motion by the action of either an individual or a group. All men seek power, in their respective ways and for their respective ends. The philosopher and the poet exercise power no less than the soldier and the sheriff. Life is a ceaseless exercise of power to effect changes for its accommodation. Of itself, power is simply a neutral agency of all change and of all stability. Professor Talcott Parsons has offered the interesting suggestion that power is a circulating medium, analogous to money, within the political system.[16] Just as a monetary system resting entirely on gold as a medium of exchange is a very primitive one, so a power system in which force is the only negative sanction is a very primitive one and must be legitimized. As we noted earlier, authority is the institutional code within which the use of power as a medium is both organized and made legitimate. Following Parsons, authority stands to power as property does to money.

The stabilization and eventual institutionalization of power is closely related to the phenomena of authority and legitimacy. The quest for power is usually justified in terms of larger

---

[16] See Talcott Parsons, "On the Concept of Political Power," in *Proceedings of the American Philosophical Society,* vol. 107, June 1963.

schemes of values. In time, however, power can become perceived as an ultimate value, transformed from a mere instrument to an end in itself.[17] History is replete with tragic accounts of men and women who became obsessed with power for the sake of power. The arrogance of power constituted a favorite theme of Greek drama. Shakespeare devoted three of his greatest plays (*Hamlet, Macbeth,* and *King Lear*) to forceful demonstrations of Lord Acton's famous dictum that "power tends to corrupt and absolute power corrupts absolutely." It can also be argued that power can ennoble those who exercise it in the interests of human welfare. A work by Rogow and Lasswell argues that power has no inherent tendency to affect an individual in any general way. Rather, the personality of each individual will determine how he will use the power he is given.[18] The institutional setting is also an important factor in conditioning the behavior of a power holder.

Nevertheless, a distinguished American sociologist, reflecting on a life of dedicated scholarship, maintains that high power inclines its owner to pay less regard to the counsel of others. Professor Robert M. MacIver bluntly asserts: "The possession of great power is prejudicial to the more kindly and humane of human qualities. . . . The possession of power magnifies the ego-weight in the scale of human values. Supreme power comes to spell supreme rightness, the approach to infallibility."[19]

While one need not argue that possession of power always corrupts, it would not be difficult to marshall a long list of individuals over every range of the power scale who have been consumed by an inordinate lust for power. On any level of authority, the power to command is suffused with temptations to play God. Professor Hans J. Morgenthau has written an essay developing the thesis that in the degree to which the aim of

---

[17] Barrington Moore, Jr., *Political Power and Social Theory* (Cambridge, Mass.: Harvard University Press, 1958), pp. 14-15.

[18] Arnold A. Rogow and Harold D. Lasswell, *Power, Corruption, and Rectitude* (Englewood Cliffs, N.J.: Prentice-Hall, 1963).

[19] Robert M. MacIver, *Power Transformed* (New York: Macmillan, 1964), especially Chapter Thirteen, "Temptations and Failings of the Mighty," pp. 189-202.

politics is power over man, politics is evil. Moreover, there is no escape from the evil of power regardless of what one does, for politics involves action and all action involves evil to some extent. Political ethics, therefore, are the ethics of doing evil; political decision-making inevitably involves the choosing of lesser evils.[20]

This brief digression on the morality of power must now yield to some concluding observations on the utility of the power analysis approach to the study of politics. The principal weakness of the power approach is its lack of precision. A concept so broad in meaning, despite its suggestion of hardness and explicitness, cannot be very clear. When it covers so many kinds of relationships and activities, a distinct handicap is imposed on the attempt to distinguish between power in general and power in a political context.

While the study of power is essential in political analysis, power is by no means confined to government and the state. There is the illegitimate power of the gangster, the hidden power of the business executive, the power of parents, priests, and even professors. Are political scientists to be concerned with the power relations of a college fraternity, a labor union, a church, a family, or a baseball team simply because there are power relationships to be found in all of them? If the answer is yes, then the task of the political scientist becomes awesome indeed. If the answer is no, then we are faced with the problem of delineating the distinctively political sphere of analysis. David Easton, in a seminal work published in 1953, attempted to narrow the focus of analysis by suggesting that political science ought to be conceived as "the study of authoritative allocation of values for a society."[21] Easton rejects the notion that all power relations, wherever they exist, automatically indicate the presence of a political situation. Rather, he would define the boundaries of political research as the attempt to understand the way in which values are authoritatively allo-

---

[20] Hans J. Morgenthau, "The Evils of Politics and the Ethics of Evil," *Ethics* (October 1945).

[21] David Easton, *The Political System* (New York: Knopf, 1953).

cated for a whole society. Hence: "Political life concerns all
those varieties of activity that influence significantly the kind
of authoritative policy adopted for a society and the way it is
put into practice."[22] Easton's definition would have the political scientist study all socially significant behavior patterns which
allocate values.

The formulation elaborated by Easton was greeted with
much interest in the profession and stimulated lively debate. It
will probably come as no surprise to the student to hear that the
words "allocation," "values," and "authoritative" were enigmatic enough to create the usual semantic disagreements. Even
those who felt that Easton's definition was a valuable contribution to the political lexicon often found themselves in serious
disagreement as to which empirical situations were to be en-
compassed by the definition.

Obviously, the usefulness and validity of the power concept is a matter for individual intellectual judgment to discern.
Like so many words in the vocabulary of political discourse,
power has not achieved the kind of precision which permits universal understanding when the term is employed by social
scientists. Although the discussion of definitions can be tedious,
in the case of power it would appear to be essential if the concept is to acquire any utility. Perhaps one of the readers of this
book can write a term paper on "Power as a Political Concept."
Should such a brave effort be made, the difficulty of attempting
to narrow the concept will be made readily apparent. Power is
an exceptionally difficult concept to define and empirically
elaborate.

The "power theorist" wishes to state causal relations between or among elements in a social or political system. He
seeks a basis for the actualities of power by isolating elements
of human relationships and projecting them into models. By
model we mean any generalized statement used to describe or
predict by stating uniformities of relationships among regularly

---

[22] *Ibid.*, p. 128.

recurring phenomena. But there is a difficulty involved in this quest which cannot be easily solved.

The power relationships institutionalized in society constitute only the visible aspect of a most complex system of social control internalized in individuals. There is an *inside* and an *outside* to every power relation. The distribution of power in a society depends on a number of external conditions, but there are important subjective conditions as well. Indeed, one could well argue that the limits of human cooperation are more fixed by these internalized controls than by the power structure of governmental arrangements or the logic of political theory. These patterns of response vary with cultural conditions; a system of political power blends many forms of social control— rational and irrational.

The greater part of the controls exerted on persons is deeply embedded in habit and conditioned responses. Pressures to conform are not totally external to behavior; they are also located in cultural components of behavior. The more traditional analysis of politics as a power phenomenon tended to overlook those pressures toward conformity that are cultural. In any power complex, political behavior patterns and institutions are particularly subject to cultural influences. The cultural perspective warns us against exaggerating the *coerciveness* of political power, for habits and customs can exert as much psychic power to promote conformity as any attempts at physical force are able to accomplish. Professor E. V. Walter has convincingly stated a case for the thesis that "ultimately, power depends on authority and voluntary obedience" and that "violence may be considered to be the failure of power."[23] Of course, coercion and consent are not mutually exclusive; they are each operative on their own. However, the significance of the power of persuasion (as opposed to the use of physical force) grows with the increasing complexity of a society.

---

[23] E. V. Walter, "Power, Civilization, and the Psychology of Conscience," *American Political Science Review* (September 1959), pp. 641-42.

The actualities of power are a *given* in all human experience, but much of that experience is exceedingly complex and defies analysis. In the modern highly organized society, the foci of power are numerous. They are kept in a moving equilibrium by the continuous processes of conflict and cooperation. Power is always limited or neutralized by opposing power. An endless interadjustment of powers characterizes modern civilization.

The generation and utilization of power constitutes one of the functional imperatives of the political system. Power becomes the focus of a set of mechanisms which become highly specialized in the institutions of advanced societies. In other words, power rests on various bases, each with a varying scope, involving decisions of import to the community. Our main problem, however, is not to determine the existence of power but to make comparisons based on the arrangement and disposition of the power structures in a given society. One hypothesis which deserves exploration is that power is cumulative: one type of power tends to adhere to other types. As a result of this coalescence, composite power structures are created, and power spreads to other fields in ever-widening circles. The merging of power structures often initiates new forms of change in society.

If we can agree that the subject matter of political science includes the study of power in human relations, we should take care to see that we do not obscure the *purposes* for which power is used or the conflict of purposes out of which politics emerges. Political actors rarely struggle for power alone. They strive for various purposes, and purpose acquires meaning only in relation to values. There is a close link among power, purpose, and values because the struggle for power is rarely divorced from purposeful motivation. Power is not a self-sufficient end but only a means toward the attainment of purposes beyond power itself. When power does become an end in itself, divorced from all meaningful motivation, we enter the realm of the pathological.

To insist that politics is a struggle for power does not tell us what price, in terms of other values, political actors are willing to pay for it. Not all power seekers gain power, perhaps because many of them are unwilling to pay the necessary price in terms of self-sacrifice and sacrifice of others. Conversely, some men who do not actively seek power may have power thrust upon them which they must exercise as wisely as they can.

In any case, the basic point must be stressed strongly: power can be used to gain a great variety of ends. Men seek power, not for its own sake, but because of its instrumental value. Once more, we can make an analogy comparing power to money. The accumulation of coins is not what an economist defines as good business; the accumulation of power as an end in itself would not be defined as "good politics" or "good morality," for that matter. Power manifests itself in action. Many people desire power because they aspire to control the means to achieve their respective ends. The quantity and quality of power used by men are determined by human purposes. Depending on the culture, society, and political system, power may be used to acquire money, fame, affection, respect, and other values. Conceptions of authority and purpose will condition the pattern of power relations in each political system. We must never neglect the effect of these influences on the actors who struggle for power.

Power itself, then, is neither good nor bad except in the way it is employed. To the political analyst, power is used strictly as a neutral, functional, and nonevaluative term, denoting a factual situation or relationship which is ethically neither good nor evil. There are many different reasons, conscious and unconscious, why men seek power; there are many variations in the costs and benefits of power from one political system to another. Some people quite obviously seek power more ardently than others, but why this is so is a matter of intellectual controversy. Both Nero and Gandhi sought power. To assert that politics is nothing but a struggle for power would fail to discriminate the specific purposes for which those two men acted. Power cannot be understood unless it is interpreted in the context of the circumstances that produce it and the ends that it serves. In many cases, purpose may be the critical difference, since man is a moral creature capable of making choices in politics as in other fields of human endeavor.

The power theory of politics can perhaps be better termed the "power hypothesis." Better still, one could say that there are various hypotheses in political science which use power as a guiding concept to orient research activities. Some students have tried to go further and use power as an operational concept in their research on the political and social system.[24] It appears clear that the student who chooses to use some formulation of the power hypothesis in his scholarly activities must rethink the concept as he faces empirical situations that challenge its traditional verbal uses. If Professor Heinz Eulau is correct in his assertion that "power is still a concept we cannot do much with apparently, but which we do not dare to do without,"[25] we shall simply have to try to define power in terms of the realms in which it operates and of the kinds of effects it can produce.

In using power in such a fashion, we must beware of falling into the single-factor fallacy. Such a "power monism" does not account for all political behavior and gives us, instead, an overly simplified, crudely mechanistic portrait of reality. Some analysts have applied the term *realism* to theories of power politics, but such "realist" theory is actually unreal when it refuses to come to terms with the factors that influence or define purposes. We have stressed the importance of authority in this discussion and, although authority may be generated by power and increased by it, authority which lasts beyond transient situations seldom springs from power alone.

Every method of detecting and analyzing power has certain advantages and disadvantages. Power is often a most complex product of other variables strikingly different in nature. The latter should be allowed their proper attention rather than submerged in the iceberg of the power concept. The iceberg meta-

---

24 See James G. March, "The Power of Power," in David Easton, editor, *Varieties of Political Theory* (Englewood Cliffs, N.J.: Prentice-Hall, 1966), pp. 39-70.

25 Heinz Eulau, *The Behavioral Persuasion in Politics* (New York: Random House, 1963), p. 29.

phor is an appropriate one, for a great deal of substance is concealed below the exterior of the observable phenomena of power. This substance must be brought to the surface for an intensive examination of its relevance to the power situation being analyzed.

We noted earlier the aphorism of Lord Acton that "power tends to corrupt." If Lord Acton had ever held a position of great power and responsibility, his contribution might have read: "Power tends to sober. . . ." Particularly in the twentieth century, with its legacy of death and destruction, the holder of political power is more often forced to restrain than indulge his power. Lyndon B. Johnson, during his tenure in the White House, was quoted as saying: "Power? The only power I've got is nuclear—and I can't use that."[26] While the statement was made during a period of temporary frustration, it illustrates a profound truth about the nature of the most massive physical power existing in the world.

Warfare on the grand scale today becomes the madness of mutual suicide. All the nuclear powers are caught in the same net: their great power is impotent in terms of the outcome of its use. Each side calls upon the other to be deterred by its striking power, yet both become more insecure in direct proportion to the increase in their own power. The survival of the world hinges on the sober, rational decision not to employ the most powerful weapons available. It will surely be one of the great ironies of world history if men finally live at peace because they have created weapons literally too powerful to use in any rational way. We conclude on this note to underline the necessity of emphasizing the purposes in terms of which power is used. Power without purpose is absurd.

---

[26] Quoted by Saul K. Padover in "The Power of the President," *Commonweal* (August 9, 1968), p. 521.

THREE

Structural-Functional Analysis

The structural-functional approach is probably the dominant trend within structural comparative analysis today. A large literature has emerged from the writings of such scholars as Talcott Parsons, Gabriel Almond, David Apter, Marion Levy, William Mitchell, and S. N. Eisenstadt. Structures and functions automatically go together since structures are the means through which functions are performed, and functions are always accomplished by means of structures. Moreover, the nature of the functions to be performed influences the form a structure will assume. Major problems arise, however, in differentiating between the relevant and the nonrelevant effects of a structure.

Structural-functional analysis provides a framework for analyzing whole systems. It stresses the interrelatedness of structures and functions within a given system and suggests that certain necessary functions must be performed if the system is to survive. Because of this orientation, structural-functional analysis involves the identification of a set of requisite functions in the particular system under investigation. Since, by definition at least, all parts of the system are making some kind of contribution, the question of the specific function served may be asked of any of them.

In the following sections, we shall attempt to condense this fairly complicated methodology into the limited dimensions of a chapter. At the heart of the approach lies the proposition that all political systems can be compared in terms of the relationship between functions and structures. All political systems, even the simplest, have political structure. If the system is surviving, the requisite functions are being performed. The attempt must be made to determine the kinds of structures through which these functions are performed.

The Nature of Structural Analysis

A fundamental assumption of structural analysis is that human beings behave in a consistent manner: they repeat their past behavior. When interactions are repeated beyond a certain point, the result is a *structure*. The "structure" of anything consists of the relatively stable interrelationships among its components. Since social and political systems are made up of the interrelated acts of people, their structures must be sought in the degree of regularity or recurrence in these acts.[1] Structure implies that there is a stable and ordered relation of parts. Structure is closely related to system: it always presupposes that there are identifiable parts and that they are arranged in some kind of pattern or design. Structure can be regarded as the static aspect of a system, its "skeleton."[2]

The term *structure* invites images of edifices occupied or awaiting inhabitants. Actually, the general concept of structure appears to have been borrowed and adapted from physics and, more extensively, from biology. The term implies that there is something solid out there to observe; yet the term is widely used in both these sciences and the humanities. We can speak of the structure of the United States Congress, the structure of the Beethoven Ninth Symphony, the structure of a Robert Frost poem, and the structure of a Siamese cat, to mention a few

---

[1] Marion J. Levy, Jr., *The Structure of Society* (Princeton: Princeton University Press, 1952), p. 57.

[2] Carl J. Friedrich, *Constitutional Government and Democracy* (Boston: Ginn, 1941), p. 181.

at random. We can even speak of the personality structure of an individual human being; earlier in this book we analyzed the concept of social structure. Marion Levy's book on structural analysis is entitled *The Structure of Society.*

If this usage sounds chaotic and confusing, it need not necessarily result in verbal anarchy. Rather, we must simply bear in mind that the term *structure* can be correctly used in widely varying contexts depending on the subject being considered. The important thing is to be able to identify the persistent relationships that make up the particular structure. It is one thing for two physicists to speak of the structure of the atom, another thing for two architects to talk about the structure of a new skyscraper, and still another thing for two political sociologists to discuss the structure of the family or the structure of the political system.[3]

Although the method of structural-functional analysis was borrowed originally from biological research, its subsequent development in the social sciences has followed a pattern of its own. As a stream of thought, it has gathered momentum and grown in strength over the past forty years. Before the Second World War, much of the work dealt with specialized concrete structures of government such as political parties, parliaments, or courts. We have earlier noted the limitations of this formalistic approach to the study of politics and need not repeat it here.

In order to endure, structures must become stable and fairly rigid. Institutions are structures, among other things, and tend to become highly organized and highly formalized. This state of affairs is a two-edged sword. On the one hand, no society whose institutions are flabby can long endure. The basic activities of a society must be carried on in a relatively orderly, continuous, and peaceful manner. The comparative rigidity of political and social institutions gives the group greater stability than its members could achieve alone. Society receives a degree of permanence. To the extent that institutions minister

---

[3] For a more detailed consideration of these points, see N. J. Demerath III and Richard A. Peterson, editors, *System, Change, and Conflict* (New York: Free Press of Glencoe, 1967).

to man's permanent and fundamental natural needs, they are agencies whereby the life of a given society is maintained and perpetuated.[4]

Positively, then, institutions knit our social life together and give it structure and organization. Negatively, institutions have a tendency to become inflexible and formalistic. They can easily develop inertia and an imperviousness to change. Their high structural organization becomes an obstacle to changes, and adaptations become difficult. The regulations and ideology are transformed into absolutes; mechanism becomes supreme and the institution becomes the victim of its own rigidity.[5]

William C. Mitchell points out that it is not possible to understand political processes without knowing the immediate environment of the action. Structure is that immediate environment.[6] It is within the political structures that all the processes of the political system take place; moreover, the extent to which a political system is structurally differentiated will affect its performance. Any particular structure may perform more than one function; in fact, in most societies, political structures tend to be multifunctional.

Structural analysis is concerned with the limits within which particular choices take place. The methodological approach inherent in structural analysis is the identification of the functional values of relevant aspects of political and social life in their relationship to the unit under analysis. Structural analysis allows us to sort out the properties of large-scale systems; it lends itself to dealing with such macrounits as countries and governments. Much comparative work in political science has been characterized by the structural method applied comparatively.[7]

---

[4] Joyce O. Hertzler, *Social Institutions* (Lincoln: University of Nebraska Press, 1946), p. 240.

[5] *Ibid.*, p. 242.

[6] William C. Mitchell, *The American Polity* (New York: Free Press of Glencoe, 1962), p. 57.

[7] There is no theoretical reason why structural analysis cannot be applied to smaller units; we noted above that individuals can be studied as personality structures. See M. G. Smith, "A Structural Approach to Comparative

David Apter points out that structural analysis can be viewed as a kind of intellectual diamond cutting. The lines, planes, and potential fractures of the unit are observed.[8] The structural analyst tries to predict how the unit under observation will respond in the face of a particular crisis or opportunity. Structural analysis is itself a comparative method, in a form that directs our attention to an analytical level of thought rather than to a purely descriptive level. The object is to see the functional meaning in many diverse activities.

Structural Requisites of Government

A *structural requisite* is defined as a pattern of action necessary for the continued existence of the unit with which it is associated. That is to say, of the broad range of activities which governments undertake, some are vitally necessary if the unit is to continue. The following five structural requisites are suggestive of what is involved in such minimal requirements for crucial concerns of government: (1) the structure of authoritative decision-making; (2) the structure of accountability and consent; (3) the structure of coercion and punishment; (4) the structure of resource determination and allocation; (5) the structure of political recruitment and role assignment.[9] If any of these structures malfunction or fail to operate, the political system will undergo drastic modification.

From a theoretical viewpoint, the empirical variations in each of these structural requisites should be the core of comparative analysis. In fact, the phenomenon of structural alternatives (that different structures in different types of systems may contribute to the satisfaction of the same functional requisites) is basic to the whole framework. The problem is to explain why one certain structure rather than another contributes to the

Politics," in David Easton, editor, *Varieties of Political Theory* (Englewood Cliffs, N. J.: Prentice-Hall, 1966), pp. 113-28.

[8] David Apter and Harry Eckstein, eds., *Comparative Politics: A Reader* (New York: Free Press of Glencoe, 1963), p. 732.

[9] David E. Apter, "A Comparative Method for the Study of Politics," in *Some Conceptual Approaches to the Study of Modernization* (Englewood Cliffs, N. J.: Prentice—Hall, 1968), p. 29.

satisfaction of a given requisite in a given political system at a given time.[10] The structural requisites lead us to the analysis of policy and its consequences.

Each society has a pattern of organization composed of the structures resulting from human interaction. Men establish a structural form when they relate themselves to each other. The value of a given structure depends on the manner in which it fulfills its function. A society is a continuous flow of operating structures. For purposes of analysis we must hold it still in order to see the arrangement of the parts and how these parts combine to form the framework of the larger system.[11]

There are five major classes of human relationship structures of which any society is composed. They are:

1. Ecological Entities: These are aggregates of people that occupy a continuous territory integrated through common social and economic activities.

2. Human Groups: Groups are units of two or more people meeting in the same environment who are influencing each other psychologically.

3. Institutional Agencies: These are the instruments for making institutions functional. They carry out activities that have been sanctioned and formalized within the society. Education, the family, government, and religion are all institutions.

4. Organizations: These are systematically arranged units of people organized to achieve specific purposes in which each person has a formally defined role.

5. Collectivities: A collectivity consists of a number of people whose behavior is specifically polarized around

---

[10]Robert T. Holt, "A Proposed Structural-Functional Framework for Political Science," in Don Martindale, editor, *Functionalism in the Social Sciences* (Philadelphia: American Academy of Political and Social Science, 1965), p. 91.

[11] The definitive treatment of institutionalization and social institutions is Talcott Parsons, *The Social System* (New York: Free Press of Glencoe, 1951), especially pp. 36-45.

some center of attraction that stimulates interaction and unity. A crowd and an audience are illustrations of the collectivity.[12]

These five relationship structures are the major mechanisms through which each society operates. Of course, specific structures are not the same in all societies. For instance, the family is an institution found in all societies, but the norms of different societies sanction various procedures for fulfilling the primary functions of bearing children and rearing them so they become normal young adults. Each society exhibits certain basic structural features; various practices can be shown to relate to these in such a way as to contribute to their persistence.[13] The problems posed by structural analysis revolve around issues of system maintenance and system development.

The Institutional Structure of the Political System

We have observed that structure consists of those stable elements in a society that may be treated as constants over time. Structure, therefore, sets limits to the adaptability of the political system. In comparative study, we seek to determine what differences or uniformities of the political *process* correspond with observable differences or uniformities of the political *structure*.[14]

Institutions tend to become specialized in accordance with the functional problems of a society. The demonstrable fact that the total society is differentiated into various major groups indicates that such differentiation is quite essential for the orderly functioning of the system. The specialization which develops

---

[12] These five major classes of human relationship structures are adapted from Walfred Anderson and Frederick Parker, *Society: Its Organization and Operation* (Princeton, N. J.: D. Van Nostrand, 1964), p. 91.

[13] Percy S. Cohen, *Modern Social Theory* (New York: Basic Books, 1968), p. 42.

[14] For a detailed analysis of this problem see Talcott Parsons, *Structure and Process in Modern Societies* (New York: Free Press of Glencoe, 1960). See, especially, Part 3, "Structure and Process in Political Systems," pp. 169-247.

within each of the major institutions is further evidence of this fact.[15]

Although institutions are the major focus of structural analysis, they are not the sole focus. Ultimately, social structures are composed of ideas, and from these ideas are derived the basic structural concepts. The structure of society and of the political system cannot be explained without fundamental attention being paid to the institutionalization of cultural patterns in the everyday lives of the citizenry. In fact, a social or political culture is constructed of such cultural elements. Just as the genes in the higher species transcend the life cycle of a particular organism, so do cultural traits transcend the viability of their host society. Culture is not only transmitted from generation to generation through learning and teaching; it is also embodied in various externalized symbols such as works of art and the printed page.[16]

If structure answers the question "How is the political system arranged?," function answers the question "What does the political system do?" *Function* refers to the dynamic aspects of the political system: its operations, processes, mechanisms, and activities. We turn now to a discussion of the uses of functionalism in contemporary political analysis.

Functionalism in Comparative Political Analysis

Functionalism was first employed as an approach to social analysis by sociologists and anthropologists. The postwar deluge of functionalism began with Robert K. Merton's *Social Theory and Social Structure*.[17] In various forms, functional analysis is an important component of models for comparative political analysis. The approach has found ready acceptance among students of non-Western political systems because it offers units

---

[15] *Ibid.*, p. 156.

[16] Talcott Parsons and Gerald M. Platt, *The American University* (Cambridge, Mass.: Harvard University Press, 1973), p. 16.

[17] Robert K. Merton, *Social Theory and Social Structure,* rev. ed. (New York: Free Press of Glencoe, 1957), p. 20.

of analysis that can be applied outside standard governmental structures of the Western type.

The Concept of Function

Although social scientists differ substantially in their use of the concept of function, they agree that our ability to explain complicated data is enhanced when we regard social structures and institutions as performing functions within various systems. Functionalism is an umbrella concept which covers a wide variety of analytic modes. Because of this variety, there is no distinctive functional approach which can be contrasted to institutional, power, or decision-making approaches.

We discussed structural requisites of government earlier. Talcott Parsons has postulated four functional requisites necessary for the survival of any social order. They are: (1) achieving collective goals; (2) systemic adaptation to the environment; (3) controlling tension within the system and providing motivation; and (4) integrating actions of its members. Societies may be functionally explained and compared according to how each of these necessary functions is performed.

The concept of function appears to have been introduced originally into social science by Herbert Spencer. In his approach to social data, the ideas of function and evolution were mutually supporting. But as Robert K. Merton says: "The word 'function' has been pre-empted by several disciplines and by popular speech with the not unexpected result that its connotation often becomes obscure. . . ."[18] Unfortunately, the term is highly ambiguous, and there are many competing terminologies which clamor for our attention. There is, obviously, no "correct" definition of *function.*[19] Functional analysis is a broadly based intellectual movement, and social scientists think of func-

---

[18] *Ibid.,* p. 20.

[19] We cannot possibly exhaust all of the subtle distinctions involved in the various vocabularies of functional analysis. Those who wish to explore in more detail the many problems involved in defining the concept will have to chart their own course in Levy, Merton, and Parsons.

tions with differing degrees of precision and conceptual rigor. A good example of an early conception of function is found in Radcliffe-Brown's work. He writes:

> The concept of function applied to human societies is based on an analogy between social life and organic life. . . . It is through and by the continuity of the functioning that the continuity of the structure is preserved. "Function" is the contribution which a partial activity makes to the total activity of which it is a part. The function of a particular social usage is the contribution it makes to the total social life as the functioning of the total social system. Such a view implies that a social system . . . has a certain kind of unity.[20]

The theories of "functionalism" were first developed in anthropology. Anthropologists such as Radcliffe-Brown were working in societies small enough to be viewed as whole entities. The idea of society as an organized whole or structure and the related idea of function was worked out by such men as Durkheim, Malinowski, and Radcliffe-Brown. In anthropology and sociology the object of functional analysis is, in the words of Robert Merton, "a standardized (*i.e.,* patterned and repetitive) item, such as social roles, institutional patterns, social processes, cultural patterns, . . . social norms, group organizations, social structure, devices for social control, etc."[21] For example, social institutions function on three planes, that is, the individual, the social, and the societal planes. Embedded in every functional analysis is some conception of the functional requirements of the entity under observation.

Many other disciplines use the term *function* in their discourse. When biologists speak of the function of an organ, the reference is to the role that the organ plays in some system of which it is a part. The biologist might say: "A function of the blood is to provide a circulating medium to carry elements of nourishment to the cells of the body." The statement identifies

---

[20] A. R. Radcliffe-Brown, *Structure and Function in Primitive Society* (London: Cohen and West, 1952), pp. 178-79.

[21] Merton, *Social Theory,* p. 50.

an objective consequence of the presence of blood for other parts of the biological system.[22]

In psychology, psychoanalysis has a strong functional orientation. Freud's functional characterization of the role of symptom formation is an illustration of this approach. In philosophy, functionalism led to the rise of pragmatism and instrumentalism. Functionalism went hand in hand with institutionalism in economic theory. Charles Darwin's principle of natural selection is replete with functional implications. His explanations of the characteristics of particular species are framed in functional terms: the system is primary, functions maintain the system, structures perform various functions.[23]

The concept of *function* has been used in the social sciences in many different ways. The varied assortment of terms used almost synonymously with "function" include purpose, aim, intention, motive, utility, and consequences. It is apparent that the concept has developed in a most uneven fashion in the social sciences.

With all of this by way of prelude, we proceed to a more specific discussion of the use of the term in the study of political science, although *function* as used in this book draws more heavily from sociology than from political science. From the huge array of available definitions, the formulation of Robert K. Merton seems the most precise and succinct. It reads as follows: "Functions are those observed consequences which make for the adaptation or adjustment of a given system; and dysfunctions, those observed consequences which lessen the adaptation or adjustment of the system."[24]

From this point of view, the meaning of function is an activity, performed by a structure, that maintains the system of which it is a part. In any given case, an entity may have both

---

[22] Ernest Nagel, *Logic Without Metaphysics* (New York: Free Press of Glencoe, 1956), pp. 247-83.

[23] Charles Darwin, *Origin of Species* (London: J. Murray, 1859) and *Descent of Man* (London: J. Murray, 1871).

[24] Merton, *Social Theory*, p. 51.

functional and dysfunctional consequences; the problem then becomes to assess the net balance of the aggregate of consequences.[25]

Note that *function* is not a synonym for *effect*. It is a subtype of effect. Functions are system relevant effects of structures.[26] Furthermore, function should be distinguished from purpose. A purpose is something subjective (*i.e.*, something in the mind of the participant in a social system), whereas a function is an objective observable consequence of action.[27] This does not imply that motives are irrelevant to action; rather it is recognition that they are not the same thing as functions or dysfunctions. A final distinction: function is more than "interaction" in a general sense. Although in everyday language we say that a thing functions when it "works," function in scientific discourse has been given a different meaning for purposes of clarity from that of simply "working."

Although it is perfectly obvious that function can only be interpreted from watching the social interaction, it goes a step beyond merely listing what occurred in terms of activity or verbal communication. The functional description must include the relevancy of this activity to the structure as a whole. That is why it is worth repeating that it is almost impossible to speak clearly of function without thinking of structure, or the organization through which functions are traced.

There is another contribution of Robert K. Merton that we should point out before closing this discussion of the concept of function. Merton has made a classical (and crucial) distinction between *manifest* and *latent* functions.[28] On the one hand, manifest functions are those whose consequences for society or any of its subsystems are intended and recognized by

---

[25] *Ibid.*

[26] Robert T. Holt, "A Proposed Structural-Functional Framework for Political Science," in Don Martindale, editor, *Functionalism in the Social Science* (Philadelphia: American Academy of Political and Social Science: 1965), p. 87.

[27] Merton, *Social Theory*, p. 24.

[28] Ibid., p. 51.

persons taking part in the system. Latent functions, on the other hand, are those consequences that are neither intended nor recognized.

The distinction between manifest and latent functions is relative, and fixed lines between the two types of functions are not always easy to draw. The functions of particular institutions may be manifest to some persons and latent to others. The distinction is significant mainly because it calls our attention to the fact that latent functions do exist, an awareness that might otherwise be overlooked without the concept to guide us.

One might logically argue that findings concerning latent functions represent a greater increment in our knowledge than findings concerning manifest functions. It is precisely the latent functions of a structure or system that are not common knowledge. Some of the things a structure does are extremely obvious. The House of Commons in Great Britain passes laws, Scotland Yard captures criminals, and the Queen names the Prime Minister. Such obvious functions of a particular structure are called its manifest functions.

Some of the things that go on in structures are not so obvious until one begins to observe the situation more carefully. These less obvious functions are the latent ones, and a search must be made to detect them. We can state flatly that there are always potential latent functions lurking behind the manifest functions exhibited by a given structure. In the light of this continuing situation, the political analyst must often become a shrewd detective in his attempt to locate latent functions hidden within the structure being investigated.

The concept of latent function also alerts the analyst to an ironical aspect of social reform. The persistence of illicit patterns of action—such as political corruption, gambling, and prostitution—can perhaps be explained in considerable measure by reference to the latent functions they serve in the social and political systems. Robert Merton has argued that political corruption, as it develops in political machines, has often served the latent function of humanizing and personalizing the operations of government structures.[29] Proposals for social reform are likely to be ineffective if the reformer does not take into account the latent functions of the structures he is seeking to change.

Activities or conditions, then, may be found to be either functional or dysfunctional, manifest or latent. Structures have manifest and latent functions as well as manifest and latent dysfunctions. This is an important distinction to bear in mind, because a wide range of structures operates latently in human affairs. Politics is a more manifest process than most other social processes, but its corrective function for many social strains is clearly latent.

Let us conclude the point by stressing that latency and manifestness are interdependent concepts. A function is capable of being latent only if another one is manifest and vice versa.[30] To discover the functions and dysfunctions of any social pattern, it is necessary to locate it in the specific social and cultural context in which it occurs. The social structure and the cultural system generate the very problems which confront the political leaders in the polity.

The Nature of Functional Analysis

Functional explanations require "the concept of a system, a statement of the rules of interaction within that system, definitions of the various 'states' of the system, a list of the functional prerequisites of the system, and some knowledge of the mechanisms by which systems function and adjust."[31] The success attained by a functional explanation will depend on the extent to which these various requirements can be fulfilled.

Functional analysis is a way of explaining social and political occurrences by indicating the nature of their functions.

---

[29] Merton develops this argument in considerable detail in *Social Theory and Social Structure*, pp. 71-82.

[30] J. P. Nettl makes this point in *Political Mobilization* (London: Faber and Faber, 1967), p. 183.

[31] Eugene Meehan, *Contemporary Political Thought* (Homewood, Ill. Dorsey Press, 1967), p. 161.

Functionalism is also a way of investigation; that is, it provides a set of scientific tools for the analysis of complex political phenomena. Functional analysis may be applied to any operating system: for our purposes, each unit and agency of government is a system of action. Activities and conditions of these units must be analyzed and evaluated in terms of their effects on the system.

A generally accepted premise of the functional approach is that no human institution or set of behavior patterns exists in a vacuum. There is always an interplay among the various elements which constitute a given system. To learn how a given system operates is to learn what the objective consequences of any one part are for another part or for the system as a whole. Functional analysis must therefore consider widely diverse situational data to discern the political problems they present.

We are attempting to look at reality in terms of structures, processes, mechanisms, and functions. In its most general usage, functionalism simply means that in analyzing some phenomena the political scientist will be concerned with the functions served by the phenomena.

The activities of the political system may be regarded as raw data. One of the major tasks of analysis is to link activities with specific functions. The functional needs of both members and system must be met; moreover, the presence of functional alternatives has very important consequences with respect to the political system.[32]

Structural-functional analysis can enrich the discipline of political science in several ways. Two political analysts have concluded that structural-functional analysis can (1) make us sensitive to the complexity of interrelationships among social and political phenomena in our analysis; (2) draw attention to the whole social system as a setting for political phenomena; (3) force consideration of the functions served by political

---

[32] William C. Mitchell, *Sociological Analysis and Politics: The Theories of Talcott Parsons* (Englewood Cliffs, N. J.: Prentice-Hall, 1967), pp. 65-68.

groups, especially latent functions. Structural-functional analysis also provides a number of frameworks for political inquiry which political scientists can employ in their empirical investigations.[33]

The English political sociologist, W. G. Runciman, also identifies three positive values which flow from functional inquiries: (1) a framework is provided for the comparative discussion of different political systems; (2) our attention is directed to causes and effects which would otherwise pass unnoticed; and (3) some of the problems of traditional political theory may be clarified.[34] Eugene Meehan has pointed out that functional explanations can fill a serious gap in our explanatory structure created by the lack of causal laws in political science.[35] Thus functional analysis offers a means of explaining a great deal of human behavior, including political behavior. Functionalism has demonstrated a descriptive value by providing for the description of more relevant phenomena than the traditional institutional analysis.

Functions of the Political System

William C. Mitchell sets forth a four-function paradigm of the political system in the following categories:

1. The authoritative specification of system goals;
2. The authoritative mobilization of resources to implement goals;
3. The integration of the system; and
4. The allocation of values and costs.[36]

If we forget about institutions and structures for a moment, and focus on what political systems actually do, we shall see that

[33] William Flanigan and Edwin Fogelman, "Functionalism in Political Science," in Martindale, *Functionalism in the Social Sciences,* p. 125.

[34] W. G. Runciman, *Social Science and Political Theory* (Cambridge: Cambridge University Press, 1963), pp. 122-23.

[35] Eugene Meehan, *The Theory and Method of Political Analysis* (Homewood, Ill.: Dorsey Press, 1965), p. 122.

[36] William C. Mitchell, *The American Polity: A Social and Cultural Interpretation* (New York: Free Press of Glencoe, 1962), p. 7.

there are similar functions which must be performed in all of them. Of course, at certain times in individual societies, one or another of these functions may appear to be more crucial than the others. For example, during times of internal strife or international conflict, the emphasis may be placed strongly on integrating the system to meet the challenges it faces. During times of relative peace and stability, the emphasis may shift to the domestic allocation of values and costs. Political mechanisms are those social processes and interactions by which decisions concerning these allocations are made and enforced.

Carl J. Friedrich, writing from a more traditional perspective, asserts that no politically organized community known to modern history lacks the following three functions: (1) rule-making; (2) dispute-settling; (3) measure-taking. Friedrich maintains that these three are the "governing functions" of the political system; each of these functions will be exercised by one or more determinate persons who play the role which the function implies. In other words, in every political system there will be found legislators, judges, and administrators.[37] Functions are thus seen as consisting of the activities of persons playing roles in the political community. The prevailing values of the community will affect the way in which the functions are exercised.

It is fruitful to look upon the components of the political system from a functional point of view, inquire into their dynamics, and examine their relationships to other subsystems of the total society. The analysis of the functions of the political system must include not only their contribution to the total social system but also their consequences for particular groups and institutions within the society.

The structural-functional approach to the analysis of political systems encourages a search for the function of every existing structure. Since by definition all parts of the system are making some kind of contribution, the question of the specific function each serves may be asked of any of them.

---

[37] Carl J. Friedrich, *Man and His Government: An Empirical Theory of Politics* (New York: McGraw-Hill 1963), p. 57.

When political structures are viewed dynamically, we consider their contribution to the total life of society: the desires they fulfill, the needs they satisfy, the procedures they standardize, and the services they render. The value of political institutions to society is measured by the importance of their functions and the efficiency with which these are accomplished. At the risk of excessive repetition, however, we must say a final time that institutions cannot be rigorously classified on the basis of a single function, for they serve many; institutions also overlap each other in the performance of functions.

The Political Process

The term *political process* has been frequently used in the literature of political science.[38] The term reflects a way of thinking about politics current among those who are preoccupied with movement and change as a significant aspect of the study of political phenomena. When we speak of the political system in action, we refer to the various processes that take place in transforming inputs into outputs.

The term *process* has been taken over into political science from the general scientific meaning of a dynamic course, or repetitive series, of operations. The working definition we shall adopt here is that of Alan Beals: "A process is a series of interlinked events which commences under certain defined conditions and which concludes under certain defined conditions."[39] Put another way, process is where the action is within the framework of a political system. Motion is the cardinal feature of the process approach to political science.

The process approach to political phenomena is concerned with the flow of attitudes and judgments, politics, decision-making, and policy itself in the authoritative regulation and

---

[38] See, in particular, Arthur F. Bentley, *The Process of Government* (Bloomington, Ind.: The Principia Press, 1949); David B. Truman, *The Governmental Process* (New York: Knopf, 1951); Jorgen Rasmussen, *The Process of Politics* (New York: Atherton Press, 1969).

[39] Alan Beals, *Culture in Process* (New York: Holt, Rinehart, and Winston, 1967), p. 6.

allocation of things of value among people and institutions within the political system.[40] Of course, we should not speak of a product of the political process in any mechanistic sense. The principal political processes are (1) cooperation, (2) accommodation, (3) conflict, (4) competition, and (5) confrontation. These processes make up the dynamic intrasystem exchanges and transactions that occupy so much of our scholarly attention.[41]

The political process may be conceived and studied in terms of parallel and competing patterns of interaction. The five processes noted above are ways of behaving that characterize the patterned relations of the political system. These major patterns of behavior are largely standardized in structures and institutions of various kinds. The cultural expression of these main forms of political relations may differ quite broadly from one society to another, but they are observable everywhere.

Structures, institutions, rules and interpretations of them are useful but inadequate for a full understanding of the political process. In fact, the organizational aspects of the political system may be overemphasized to a point where they obscure rather than illuminate the actual trend of the real governmental process. An analysis of this process requires a careful look at the types of controls which are employed in social action.

David Easton has lucidly summarized the essence of the process approach:

> The term political process refers to a method of interpreting phenomena as much as to the phenomena themselves. It suggests that all life is a pattern of interaction among social groups and individuals and that one aspect of this interaction relates to specifically political matters. Its orientation is towards the activity taking place in a political situation. . . . It also suggests that the various social units which act (each reacts on the other) ultimately shape

---

[40] See John S. Gibson, "The Process Approach," in Donald H. Riddle and Robert E. Cleary, editors, *Political Science in the Social Studies* (Washington D. C.: National Council for the Social Studies, 1966), p. 65. Much of my discussion of the process approach is derived from that essay.

[41] William C. Mitchell, *Sociological Analysis and Politics: The Theories of Talcott Parsons* (Englewood Cliffs, N. J.: Prentice-Hall, 1967), p. 127.

the policy that emerges for the whole society. . . . Its crucial significance is, therefore, that it conceives of political life, not as the
product of any one force . . . but as the product of multiple
causes.[42]

We must go beyond the institutional structures to the
activities which give them life. Easton points out three important premises involved in the idea of a political process: (1)
policy arises out of a situation consisting of the interaction of
various social elements; (2) policy is not a final product but an
aspect of the ongoing interaction among the various elements
of the social situation; (3) there is a vast variety of activity
involved in political situations; that of the persons within the
governmental and party structure is only a manifest and small
part, when compared with the importance of nongovernmental
social groups.[43]

Both behavioral and nonbehavioral scholars are concerned
with politics as process. The political process is the mainspring
of the governing process and is in constant motion throughout
the political system. One of the important dimensions of the
process approach has been to highlight the sequential nature of
political and social phenomena. The process approach alerts us
to be on guard against overly static interpretations of political
life. To use a rather simple metaphor, we must view the political
system as a succession of frames on a movie film rather than as
a single snapshot. For analytical purposes we must, at times,
hold society still in order to view the arrangement of its parts
and how they combine to form the larger system. Once we have
learned to visualize the political system "at rest" we must not
forget to continue to study how the system functions in operation; this is where the process approach lends us its theoretical
utility. The most significant aspect of the process of governing
is that the process itself never ends.

---

[42] David Easton, *The Political System*, (New York: Knopf, 1953), p. 160.
[43] Ibid., p. 172.

FOUR

The Comparison of Total Political Systems

The term *political system* has become increasingly common in the field of comparative politics. The concept has acquired wide currency because it directs our attention to the entire scope of political activities within a society. Older terms such as *state, government,* and *nation* were restricted by their legal and institutional meanings. Adopting the concept of political system allows us to broaden the scope of comparative politics to include the whole range of political systems which exist in the modern world. Students using a systems approach to political life have consciously oriented their approaches to analyzing the characteristics all political systems have in common.

There are difficult problems of terminology to be grappled with in the following discussion. The very concept of system is simply not amenable to a precise and unambiguous definition. One problem is that systems theory has progressed mainly in social sciences other than those concerned with politics. It is only recently, under the influence of the behavioral approach, that its use has been advocated by political scientists. The origins of general systems theory began with the thinking of a biologist, Ludwig von Bertalanffy, in the 1920s. But little was done in the area until after the Second World War, when a number of people began to write in various disciplines about the unification of scientific knowledge.

The trend toward generalized theories is taking place in many fields and in a variety of ways. Political science is no exception to this generalization. Those who are working in systems theory argue that the system concept is equally relevant to every science, a kind of scientific common denominator which sharpens and expands our knowledge in an integrative way. Physics, biology, mathematics, ecology, psychology, economics, sociology, and political science are all within the orbit of systems theory analysis. The relevant vocabulary is often cross-disciplinary, such as "feedback" and "equilibrium."

The originators of general systems theory believe that a great variety of disciplines in the natural and social sciences must deal at a basic level with systems of one kind or another. There are certain fundamental concepts relevant to systems of all kinds. The theory attempts to give a coherent picture of diverse fields and to provide some unity in explanation. James G. Miller, for example, asserts nineteen hypotheses which he claims to be "testable empirically at the levels of cell, organ, individual, small group and society."[1] This is system-building with a vengeance!

The student of political science must ask himself the following question: Can political life be regarded as a system? If so, what sort of system? If not, to what extent is it profitable to treat it *as if it were*? The remainder of our discussion in this chapter will be devoted to the intellectual implication and application of an affirmative response to that first question. We shall also examine the arguments of those scholars who question the purposes and methods of systems analysis.

Systems analysis attempts to depict political life as a system in which all the parts are functionally related in a kind of regular and self-consistent universe. The point of departure for theoretical analysis of this nature assumes that political inter-

---

[1] James G. Miller, "Toward a General Theory for the Behavioral Sciences," *American Psychologist,* vol. 10 (1955), p. 525.

actions in a society constitute a system of behavior. The task of analyzing a political system consists in the characterization of all the various patterned interactions which take place within it.

A *system* implies the interdependence of parts and a boundary of some kind between it and its environment. Any collection of real objects that interact in some way with one another can be considered a system, whether it be a football team or a political party. The interdependence of parts implies that when the properties of one component in a system change, all the other components are affected. The notion of boundary implies that a system starts somewhere and stops somewhere. The boundaries of political systems are subject to relatively large expansions and contractions. They are greatly extended during times of war; with the return to more normal conditions in peacetime, they contract. The boundary of a political system obviously involves more than mere geography.

The more clearly the characteristic features of the political system can be described and defined, the greater the possibility of valid comparison between different political systems becomes. We must understand at least four major concepts: system, environment, feedback, and response.[2] Let us examine these four orienting concepts in some detail.

1. *The Concept of System*

As noted earlier, the concept of a system can be used in different ways. Perhaps the two most common ways it has been employed are as a conceptualization of organic structure or as a mechanical structure. The comparison of social and political systems to living organisms has been frequently rejected as naive and purely metaphorical. But only one assumption is required in order to accept the analogy: namely, that *some* degree of determinism exists in human affairs. The analogy is not merely allegorical if real similarities can be traced between the

---

[2] See David Easton, *A Framework for Political Analysis* (Englewood Cliffs, N. J.: Prentice-Hall, 1965), p. 25.

functioning of living organisms and of political systems (such as growth and evolution).

As for the mechanistic use of the concept, a similar argument obtains. A mechanism may be defined as any arrangement or structure of acts and responses that makes possible the attainment of certain functions or needs. The concept of mechanism is used in the social sciences to designate the arrangement of parts and processes by means of which specified ends or goals are achieved. A mechanism could be an institution, a pattern of culture, a group structure, or any of dozens of acts and responses. The structure of the system sets its needs, and various mechanisms are employed to pursue these objectives. So long as we avoid the error of talking as if systems had a compulsive will of their own, the mechanistic conception of system may be useful in social analysis.

Regardless of the context, then, the concept of system postulates a set of things related in some way, so that changing any one thing in the set will make a difference to other things in the system. Systems with human beings as the parts are generally known as social systems. One kind of social system is a political system. The important point to remember in all of this is that the idea of system with regard to political life provides a starting point that is heavily weighted with consequences for a whole pattern of analysis.

2. *The Environment of a Political System*

As David Easton puts it: "A system is distinguishable from the environment in which it exists and open to influences from it."[3] This rather simple declaration contains a great many implications which are crucial for political analysis. Political phenomena must cope with the problems generated by exposure to influences from the surrounding environment. Naturally, no system of any kind functions in a vacuum; a system is open to influences from its environment. In order to determine what lies within a particular system and what falls outside it, we must

---

[3] Ibid., p. 24.

specify the boundaries of that system. This task may be relatively simple or extremely difficult for the following reasons. Boundaries are usually assigned to a political system by convention. Such conventional boundaries are often geographical in nature. We have maps of various societies and the boundaries on these maps unquestionably represent positive restrictions on the behavior of people in the respective political units. Describing geopolitical boundaries does not exhaust the other boundaries which surround the political system. What is the nature of these boundaries? It is of crucial theoretical significance in this regard to stress that, in addition to the physical environment, the political system must be visualized as surrounded by biological, social, cultural, and psychological environments. The political system lies exposed to influences deriving from the other systems in which it is embedded.

Notice, then, that one can quite accurately and precisely refer to part of the social environment that lies *outside* the boundaries of a political system and yet *within* the same society. We can refer to changes that occur in social systems other than the political system. For example, an economic depression, a shift in the social class structure, or a change of cultural values may each have great consequences for the political system. Although these changes occur in areas outside the normal confines of the political system, they nevertheless take place within the same society as that which contains the political system.[4]

The way a political system behaves is also influenced by the existence of other political systems. Although one might be able to think of a small, completely isolated tribe somewhere on the face of this planet, the vast majority of political systems do not exist in such isolation. Every political system engages in foreign relations and must take into account the behavior of other political systems in its decision-making process.

The problem of boundaries assumes significance because systems theory generally divides interaction processes into three phases: input, conversion, and output. The inputs and outputs

---

[4] Ibid., p. 71.

involve the political system with other social systems. Transactions are made between the system and its environment. We can talk about the sources of inputs, their number and content, and how they enter the political system. Similarly, we can discuss the number and content of outputs and how they emerge from the political system and affect other social systems. We are, in effect, talking about the boundaries of the political system. We have a model of the political system as an input-output process, involved with interactions with surrounding environments and responding in a more or less adaptive manner to these environments.

The approach described here suggests that what is occurring in the environment affects the political system through the kinds of influences that flow into the system. Through its structures and processes, the system acts on these intakes in such a way that they are converted into outputs. We can study this vast conversion process in its complexity as it acts upon the demands that are made upon it. In the terminology of David Easton, this process of converting inputs into outputs results in the authoritative allocation of values for the society. The making of binding and authoritative decisions distinguishes the political system from other systems both within and without the overall society that forms the environment of the political system.

Input-output analysis treats all political systems as both open and adaptive systems. The central focus of the approach is on the nature of the exchanges and transactions that take place between a political system and its environment. Political activities constitute "a system of behavior embedded in an environment to the influences of which the political system itself is exposed and in turn reacts."[5]

Various demands are made upon the political system. We shall examine some of them in more detail at a later point. Here it suffices to say that these demands go through a long con-

---

[5] David Easton, *A Systems Analysis of Political Life* (New York: John Wiley and Sons, 1965), p. 18.

version process before reaching the output stage in a political system. The conversion process is a weeding-out procedure: many demands are articulated but relatively few can reach the output stage.

Input-output analysis is simply a framework for conceptualizing, organizing, and manipulating data. It subsumes ecological, biological, personality, and social systems to be explored as major external systems of importance. The approach systematizes the study of relationships between a system and its total environment.

3. *The Concept of Feedback*

Let us attempt a brief definition of feedback as a major orienting concept in systems analysis. *Feedback* means a communications network that produces action in response to the input of information, and includes the results of its own action in the new information by which it modifies its subsequent behavior. A simple feedback network contains arrangements to react to an outside event in a specified manner until a specified state of affairs has been attained. A political system is endowed with feedback and the capacity to respond to it.

In its application to politics, the feedback concept permits a sophisticated approach to dealing with the way in which members of a political system cope with stress. The kind of role that feedback plays in enabling a system to cope with its environment or to achieve its goals will vary with the kind of system under consideration. Not all systems have the same capacity to cope with their environment.

Norbert Wiener defined feedback as "the property of being able to adjust future conduct by past performances."[6] If it were not for feedback, the behavior of a system could not take into account past experiences nor future events. It could not learn from its own successes and errors. With feedback, a system is able to attain some idea of how close it has come to its objec-

---

[6] Norbert Wiener, *The Human Uses of Human Beings* (New York: Doubleday Anchor Books, 1954), p. 33.

tives; it is in a position to modify its behavior according to what it has "learned." Feedback enables the members of the system to learn to know themselves and the situation in which they are involved.

The overall performance of a political system will depend to a great extent upon the interplay of feedback factors in the political process. The political system must be guided, at least in part, by information concerning its own performance in the past. The system must receive information about goals and respond to such information by changes in its behavior when alterations are indicated. Feedback permits the continuous revision of long-range hopes and possibilities. It is through these feedback processes that political systems adapt to changes in their environments.

In our discussion of the decision-making approach, we emphasized the importance of information in that process. Feedback obviously plays a crucial role in decision-making. The system must provide some means for bringing to the attention of its decision centers accurate information about the state of the system and its environment. This information can then be compared with what had been anticipated and taken into account in any future action.

Of course, feedback can be ignored by the authorities. When this happens, their effectiveness may be seriously impaired by their failure to find out what was happening. Feedback is fundamental both for error regulation and for redirection toward new goals when existing ones are found wanting. Without feedback, uninformed guesswork and sheer intuition would prevail in the political system. If feedback is delayed or distorted, the effects would be negative in character. Delay can be deadly; distortion is dysfunctional. One can think of exceptions to this abbreviated diagnosis, but not very many. The ones conjured up are usually examples which embody highly unusual situations which are hardly the guiding norm of behavior.

The exploration of the operations of the feedback process in a political system is of vital significance. Anything that serves to delay, distort, or disrupt the flow of information to the authorities interferes with their capacity to take action on problems confronting the system. We might investigate, for instance, whether democratic systems possess something special in their feedback processes that enable them to cope with problems and stresses which emerge from the surrounding environment. The way in which the authorities may be expected to cope with feedback responses will be a function of the kind of experiences transmitted to them through their culture. Systems tend to build up a pattern of responses to situations that influence succeeding generations.

Mechanisms of a feedback nature are at the basis of purposeful behavior in political and social systems. In order to assess the results of a flow of decisions, one must be able to state the goals or purposes toward which the decisions aim. Raising questions concerning outcomes leads us to a consideration of such factors as compliance and effectiveness. The processes of goal-seeking are important because political systems sometimes face situations in which their original goals have been altered in the context of political operations.

Feedback plays a more significant role in those systems that are able to select from a broad range of alternative responses. The outputs are purposive, rather than random. On the basis of feedback a political system is capable of reorganizing its behavior; it can modify its purposive patterns or goals by recommitting its resources.[7]

4. *The Concept of Response*

Professor Easton defines *response* as: "Variations in the structures and processes within a system . . . interpreted as constructive or positive alternative efforts by members of a system to regulate or cope with stress flowing from environmental as well as internal sources."[8] Systems must have the capacity to respond to disturbances and thereby adapt to the situations in

---

[7] Easton, *A Systems Analysis*, p. 371.
[8] Easton, *A Framework for Political Analysis*, p. 25.

which they find themselves. Not all disturbances need strain the system but many will lead in the direction of stress.

Political systems are subject to influences of many kinds coming to them either from the environment or from within. Even under conditions of stability, interaction between the system and its environment continues to occur. Members of the system are not merely passive transmitters of things taken into the system; they are able to regulate, modify, and innovate in response to the flow of inputs into the system. These responsive actions may lead to the development of new sets of circumstances that can be probed analytically.

A system must have the institutions or other means to cope with disturbances and stresses within it. In addition, it must have the mechanisms to time its actions appropriately in order to achieve maximal results from actions that are taken. Systems develop a number of different kinds of responses as they persist through time. Through the way a system structures its regime, a range of alternatives is available from which it may select its responses. In fact, political systems accumulate large repertoires of mechanisms by which they attempt to cope with their environments. Through these mechanisms, they may regulate their own behavior, transform their internal structure, and remodel their fundamental goals.

We spoke earlier of demands which are made upon the political system. The concept of *demands* is central to systems analysis and is defined as "an expression of opinion that an authoritative allocation with regard to a particular subject matter should or should not be made by those responsible for doing so."[9] Demands may be categorized in a variety of ways. Almond and Powell list four kinds of demands that confront the political system: (1) demands for allocation of goods and services, such as demands for educational opportunities, wage and hour laws, roads; (2) demands for the regulation of behavior, such as provisions for public safety and rules pertaining to health and sanitation; (3) demands for participation in the

---

[9] Easton, *A Systems Analysis*, p. 38.

political system, such as the right to vote, hold office, and organize political associations; (4) demands for communication and information, such as demands for the affirmation of norms and displays of political power on behalf of the system in periods of danger or on ceremonial occasions. A political system faces these demands in many combinations, forms, and degrees of intensity.[10]

Those who voice the demands presume that persons normally perceived as responsible for the daily business of acting on behalf of society will take the desired actions. Following Easton's formulation, demands assume a political system in which an effort is made to bring the weight of society on one's side. Demands are postulated as central variables because without them there would be no occasion to undertake the making of binding decisions for a society. The reason for this is simple: without some inflow of demands there would be no raw material for the system to process and no conversion work for it to do. No incentives would exist to spark decisions and action on the part of the political system.

Conflicts over demands constitute the flesh and blood of all political systems. A political system in which the input of demands shrank to zero would be a system in disintegration. There would be no reason for its existence except as a cultural curiosity. Without the assertion of demands the politically dominant members of a system could not orient themselves to the major problems requiring their attention. Moreover, in all political systems, some individual or some group must be able to assert that this (whatever) ought to be done or this ought to be done in this way. To respond, the person or group in authority must have some range of alternatives from which a selection may be made.

We have seen that a political system exists in multiple environments, and focusing on demands is a theoretical way of linking events in any one of these environmental systems to the political system; however, one should not ignore the many in-

---

[10] Gabriel Almond and G. Bingham Powell, Jr., *Comparative Politics: A Developmental Approach* (Boston: Little, Brown, 1966), pp. 25-26.

fluences and demands that originate within the political system itself. Easton refers to such "inbred" demands by using the term *withinputs* to distinguish them from the inputs which arise from outside the political system. The latter are shaped by such parameters as culture and social structure, whereas the "withinputs" are politically determined.

An Evaluation of Systems Theory

A number of criticisms of systems theory have appeared in recent years. We can only highlight a few of the evaluations of this methodology in order that the student may have a general idea of the issues at stake in the discussion of the utility of this schema.

Perhaps the most common criticism of systems analysis is that the conceptual categories lead the user of such theories to force all phenomena into the framework of the system. Furthermore, the boundaries between the political system and other systems are said to be ambiguous. There seems to be a hidden assumption in systems theory of a *necessary* interdependence of parts and automatic processes. This assumption may stem from the analogy between society and a biological organism, yet this analogy is highly suspect. Human societies differ from both physical systems and living organisms. The fact that societies are systems composed of human beings and of a much smaller number of components makes them qualitatively different from physical systems. More specifically, the parts of the human body necessarily have to hang together, and there is a greater presumption that they function together than there is in the case of a society, in which the several segments can go off in different directions and have great separation from each other.

It is this business of misplaced analogies that has drawn the fire of a great many critics of system theory. The critics tend to believe that the self-conscious borrowing from biology, physics, and other sciences tends to lure the political scientist into traps that are concealed by misplaced analogies. The issue here seems to lie between those who regard certain analogies as significant and those who are suspicious of the analogies.

Opinions will continue to differ on such matters until the utility of the analogy is demonstrated in an empirical way; the question can hardly be resolved on an abstract or deductive basis.

Some observers find it difficult to discover precisely what the systems theorists hope to achieve. Granting the usefulness of some of the analogies drawn, critics maintain that systems theorists fail to say anything about what the analogy is supposed to prove or suggest (while nevertheless implying that something profound has been suggested or proved).

Although a frequently stated goal of systems analysis is the use of "hard-science" methodology, some critics assert that metaphysical speculation plays a large role in formulating many of the theses of the approach. The charge is made that the development of highly abstract categories has a seductive attraction for its own sake: what emerges is a collection of verbal categories which wind up as empty file drawers. Barrington Moore, Jr., has characterized this intellectual activity as the "new scholasticism."[11] He regards much of this formal deductive model-building as splitting verbal hairs with an axe. He concludes that until it can prove its utility on much more concrete materials, systems theory will continue to resemble a theology more than a system of scientific discourse.

The question of whether systems analysis constructs an elephant gun to kill a mouse has also been debated. Criticism has been aimed at the extreme complexity of the presentation of the analytic schemes of such writers as David Easton.[12] This

---

[11] For a complete elaboration of this skepticism, see Barrington Moore, Jr., "The New Scholasticism and the Study of Politics," *World Politics,* vol. 6 (October 1953).

[12] The highly condensed presentation of the systems analysis approach of David Easton presented in this chapter is quite inadequate, but in the space permitted here such an abbreviated version was necessary. The interested reader should turn to *A Framework for Political Analysis* and *A Systems Analysis of Political Life* for the complete exposition of this new general theory of political interaction. Since the latter work is over five hundred pages in length, it is obvious that a great deal of effort is required to master the theoretical model which Easton has constructed. The approach is one of the few systemic frameworks originally developed by a political scientist rather than adapted for political analysis from some other discipline.

does not imply a denial of the value of such a framework as a valid working tool, but rather suggests that its value to the political science discipline is endangered by dedication to an overwhelming array of extremely complicated definitions and formulations. One might also add that competent scholars have long sought answers to most of the questions raised in the scheme, even though their research product has not been couched in the same rigorous vocabulary or framework.

While it can readily be granted that knowledge can be gained by studying political systems as operating wholes, it is not so clearly evident that one needs to adopt the vocabulary of systems theorists for this worthy purpose. One can study political systems without also studying the solar system, ant colonies, atoms, and the human body. It is true that systems theorists aim at high levels of generality, but so do other theorists. There is nothing invidious about abstraction as such, because there are times when it is necessary to raise the level of abstraction in order to give meaning and content to a group of variables that do not appear significantly related when discussed at a lower level of abstraction. As we noted in our earlier discussion of concepts, the very breadth of a high-level conceptualization may project a certain ambiguity. Theories of the political system which entail a high level of abstraction do not readily lend themselves to the needs of empirical research. They are remote from reality. This lack of concern for the substance of politics and the implied norms of stability lead the systems theorist almost inevitably to a manipulative approach.

The excessive preoccupation with stability in so much of the literature on systems theory has also been criticized. The view of the system as a self-sufficient, internally consistent mechanism in which a state of equilibrium is construed as the governing norm for the health of the system, presents a static image, whereas the law of life is continuous change. Stability is only one of several basic goals pursued by political systems; systems theory, with its built-in bias toward stability, cannot capture the inherent dynamism of the simultaneous political processes that interact to form the context of political life.

Of course, the terms *stability* and *change* are altogether relative. Nothing in political relationships and processes is static. The question is the particular quality of a system which is emphasized in a research posture. Critics of systems analysis maintain that change rather than equilibrium is the *normal* state of affairs. Systems analysis does not deal effectively with this reality.

This controversy seems bootless for the following reasons. Any kind of social or political analysis must grapple with processes taking place over a period of time; different approaches will order and interpret their observations in various ways. To see a society as an operating whole (as in systems theory) is surely not to portray it as standing still. Within any political system there will be found processes of varying degrees of complexity, more or less regular sequences of events in which men conform to established norms and fit into existing social structures.

Political communities are capable of changing. Stability may mean that change tends to occur at a slow pace, but the term *slow* is relative. The problem of political stability is one of the major problems of political theory. We can talk of stable or orderly change and unstable or disorderly change. Very basic changes can occur in the structure of some political systems without seriously endangering their stability. In others, seemingly small changes in one area or another may threaten the system itself.

A social or political system may change at varying rates, in various respects, and in a variety of ways, but systems never change at one rate, in one way, and in all respects. They are never one thing to the exclusion of all else. The failure to distinguish between various kinds of change is a serious flaw in any theoretical formulation. We must, therefore, specify the basic objects with regard to which changes occur in the system. We must make a valiant effort, in the face of enormous complexity, to understand political change in great detail and attempt to account for it in meaningful terms. The first step in this direction is to realize the wide variety of forms that change can take in the interaction of social and political systems.

Since change takes place through a variety of processes,

its repercussions are felt throughout the political system. Some-times the most significant political phenomena are changes in the temper of the times which may resist empirical formulations, since moods are difficult to conceptualize and categorize. Most changes in the political system are probably the product of human agents; human beings are aware of goals and the ob-stacles to those goals which must be overcome. Political systems reflect man's consciousness of the possible; various changes are given priority as people expand their awareness of desirable human values to be realized through political means.

Adopting a concept of equilibrium does not necessarily rule out conflict within the system. One can, indeed, conceive of a political system as one whose equilibrium is constantly being disturbed and in some degree reestablished. Since no system is absolutely static, this equilibrium can be described as dynamic or moving. As changes occur, adjustments are made that tend to restore the equilibrium of the system. If appropriate adjust-ments are not made, the system may begin to disintegrate. There is nothing automatic about such adjustments, of course. They may be avoided or delayed for a long time, leading to pres-sures which explode in violence or drastic changes. When that happens a new integration may result, differing in many impor-tant respects from the old order.

We shall not tarry longer over the question of the relative importance of studying stability and change. Since both change and stability are all around us, one would think that both are worthy of intensive analysis. People react to change and stabil-ity in different ways. Perhaps a person reveals a large portion of his politics and personality by revealing whether he prefers change or stability (and what kinds of change he prefers, if any).

If a theorist adopts an intellectual posture which, in effect, asserts that the factors in society which contribute to agreement and harmony are fundamentally more important than those which create conflict and disagreement, that is his prerogative. This, however, is an assumption which precedes and cannot be deduced from the analysis of the phenomena he undertakes to describe and evaluate. Such assumptions can never be proved: like all philosophical standpoints, they can only be well or ill defended. These are simply cases of rival interpretations of human actions which place prior emphasis and value on certain normative elements of the social or political system. In this sense, every scheme of analysis has certain "conceptual priorities," explicit or implicit.

Conflict and integration are inseparable. Political systems are concerned with both. Interesting and important questions flow from these conceptual bedfellows. How is it possible that some political systems (such as the entire system of China from the sixth century until well into the eighteenth) last for a long time? On the other hand, why is it that all political systems (as Plato pointed out) invariably change with the passage of time? There are various theories about aspects of change and stability as applied to the study of political systems. An adequate modern system theory will seek to account for these processes and attempt to determine the degree of their constitutive importance in the political system.

Professor K. William Kapp has argued that human society may be understood as a system composed of a network of four interacting substructures. They are:

1. The system of institutionalized arrangements related to the procreation and enculturation of the young and to the transmission of man's acquired experiences and propensities.

2. The system of institutionalized arrangements related to the production and distribution of goods and services required or desired for the gratification of human wants.

3. The system of institutionalized arrangements related to the substitution of collective (public) power and coercion for private power and coercion.

4. The system of thought, value orientations, art, religion, and ritual performances which are shared and

transmitted and which channel human action and responses into more or less regular and stable performances and strivings.[13]

Since these four substructures are connected by a process
of continuous interaction, any modifications in one must lead
to a transformation of the whole. Innovations are possible in
each of the four substructures. Social change and social structure are not contradictory; the latter includes the former, but
the presence of human purposes tends to make the relationships between the components of social systems more complex
than the characteristics of biological structures. Human society,
including the political system, is in a continuous process of
change and development in which new institutional arrangements and novel social structures continually arise.

The relative newness of systems analysis in political inquiry makes assessment of its merits difficult in some respects.
The approach may very well turn out to be a fruitful mode of
discourse which will meet the need for a systematic interrelation
of variables and provide unity in explanation of political phenomena. It remains to be seen whether efforts to develop a
systems analysis of political life will prove useful. The utility of
its conceptualization must be demonstrated with reference to
empirical work. The systems approach has not yet been applied
extensively and in detail in empirical political research. Some
of its advantages and disadvantages will show up more clearly
with the growth of a body of applications. We shall simply have
to wait and see.

Limitations of Models

Any theoretical model, whether of systems analysis or
other types of inquiry, involves a choice of variables. Models
become models by excluding some variables to concentrate on
others. Their relevance to reality depends on the importance of
the included variables in the world from which they are taken.

---

[13] K. William Kapp, *Toward a Science of Man in Society* (The Hague:
Martinus Nijhoff, 1961), p. 114.

This exclusion is not a defect but rather a virtue. A model is a simplification, not a reproduction, of reality. The virtue of simplification becomes a vice only if the model builder is unaware of his exclusions, or forgets about them and attempts to apply conclusions drawn from the model directly to human behavior.

If the analyst does forget the nature of his model, he will be in danger of playing an intellectual game with entities which have no existence outside his fantasy and have no relevance for the comprehension of reality. The danger of formal models is that they can very easily become a triumph of form over substance. Perhaps the most important objection to the use of freely invented constructs derives from the fact that they make it particularly easy to evade the empirical test and thereby contribute to the survival of false propositions in the social sciences. The more abstract the model, the easier it becomes to evade disproof by erecting a self-sealing theoretical system that loses any relationship to particular social contexts.

All working models must be used with common sense and the recognition that they are simply convenient abstractions. Ideal types and mathematical models are no substitute for the substantive study of the complex interrelationships of social structures. Substantive study uses abstractions which remain connected with the world of experience. The political scientist must be much more skeptical in his use of fictitious constructs and formal analysis than the physicist.

Scientific study, especially comparative analysis, is the attempt to find recurrent relationships which permit us to predict regularities in the real world. It may be necessary to dismember reality, but in doing so we should never lose sight of the fact that our central concern is with the actual problems of human behavior, human needs, and social processes. The substantive problems of man's interaction with his various environments must be both the point of departure and the goal of any integrated political inquiry. Metaphors may aid in the process of creative thought about political systems, but they must not become categorical imperatives.

Individuals, groups, and societies are streams of historical events which, unlike the models abstracted from them, take place in nonrecurrent situations. In the natural sciences, the most relevant features appear to be repetitive. In the social sciences, repetitiveness can be postulated only by abstracting from relevant features which combine in fact into unique situations. In the social sciences, we can only isolate the relevant variables in our analytical models. All social systems and social processes manifest unique complexity; nevertheless, there *are* regularities in human affairs, and there *are* organizing relationships in social and political systems which can be subjected to verification. Life may be indeterminate but few would assert that it is utterly chaotic. Neither natural nor social science could proceed from such an assumption. There are, indeed, definite limits on the possibilities of accurate prediction, but they do not rule out general estimates of the direction of change. Even so, very few political scientists are under the illusion that their discipline can ever be as conclusive in its propositions as, say, physics. The methods by which hypotheses are obtained and checked vary from one discipline to another, because the kind of knowledge which one can hope to achieve varies from field to field. There is no imperative reason why prediction *must* become the touchstone of adequate theory. It depends on the nature of the subject matter being investigated. Some data are more predictable than other data by their very nature. Quantification is more appropriate to some areas than to others. Aristotle's injunction is still most relevant today: "It is the mark of an educated man to look for precision in each class of things just so far as the nature of the subject matter permits."[14]

Every scientific statement is a hypothetical description of what are believed to be observed phenomena. The more recurrent the phenomena, the more generalized the description can become. Different approaches can be applied to various subsets of relevant questions. In setting up a particular problem for in-

---

[14] Quoted by Carl J. Friedrich in *Man and His Government: An Empirical Theory of Politics* (New York: McGraw-Hill, 1963), p. 8.

vestigation, it is most important to consider first the subject area one desires to analyze and the kinds of questions for which answers would be most useful. One can then consider various approaches in terms of their comparative utility in dealing with the questions which have been posed. There should be some flexibility in matching approaches to substantive questions for analysis.

All of us inhabit two worlds simultaneously: the orderly conceptual world and the untidy existential world. The differences, which are quite fundamental, may be taken as a point of departure for the construction of any conceptual scheme of analysis. Somehow, the conceptual world must be elaborated in such a way as to illuminate the tangible world of political reality. The position of the social scientist is distinguished by the elements of indeterminacy which are so prominent in the material with which he deals. The world of human society is artificial by contrast with the natural world that obeys the laws of nature. Social organization represents human artifice; that artifice is free to produce developments in a multitude of directions without the hindrance of any narrow limits set by a natural order. Politics, then, is the mediation between the conceptual and the existential worlds.

The existence of a multiplicity of approaches is basically a healthy sign of vitality in comparative studies. Furthermore, coexistence among a variety of approaches is the constructive response to this pluralism, as opposed to the kind of mentality which would seek to establish a methodological orthodoxy by elevating certain concepts and approaches to the level of intellectual dogmas. Where there is only one right answer, one may assume that only one correct question has been asked.

There is a real sense in which any approach can become an ideological prison. Dogmatic commitment to one approach or conceptual scheme reduces the analyst's freedom to follow a more flexible, eclectic intellectual path. Although there is no intrinsic merit in eclecticism of the kind which borrows from several approaches and spawns a methodological bastard of dubious utility, there is a good deal of rather convincing empirical evidence that an open-minded eclecticism has produced our best work to date, and there is good reason to believe that this will remain true in the indefinite future. Scientific research is a series of successive approaches to truth, comparable to the exploration of an unknown land. Each explorer checks and adds to the findings of his predecessors, facilitating for his successors the attainment of the goal they all have in common. In political science, that common goal is the attainment of reliable knowledge about political life.

An ideological thrust toward doctrinal purity creates an atmosphere in which there is little interest in exploring the connections among approaches, let alone attempting to utilize them in a complementary way. The optimum strategy would seem to be the eclectic selection of approaches on the basis of the requirements of a given piece of substantive research. Rigid adherence to a single approach for all purposes inhibits innovation and creativity.

Explanation of political events is likely to remain partial and nonpredictive, on balance. How could it be otherwise in a subject which deals with living human beings in all of their complex humanity? Scholars will differ, as always, in their descriptions and explanations of the political world they examine. How objective or scientific can political analysis be (and become)? What role do values play in political inquiry? In the next chapter we shall examine some of the controversy which swirls around these questions, including the challenges posed by behavioral science for the future of political inquiry.

FIVE

Comparative Politics and Political Theory

Political theory in the sense of a systematic formulation of political concepts is very old. Once more we can go back to Aristotle, whose writings contain complex theoretical notions about political life. It has been said of Aristotle that he was the first significant scholar in the West to treat facts seriously. His intellectual mentor, Plato, was the first writer who reflected systematically on politics at all. A convenient oversimplification is to say that while Plato was the first political philosopher, Aristotle was the first known political scientist.

Regardless of the labels we attach to their work, both Plato and Aristotle are important because of what they tell us about political life in fourth century B.C. Greece. The theory and practice of Greek politics is preserved in their writings. They were the first thinkers to present the idea of a scientific method in politics. They were pioneers in suggesting that the phenomena of political life are linked together by underlying patterns and principles which could be observed and reasoned about in intellectual discourse.

Most students of the history of Western political thought begin their accounts with the philosophers of the Greek city-state.[1] They may bring their studies right up to the twentieth century and contemporary political thought. Employing an historical approach, they discuss the fundamental philosophies of the major political theorists from Plato to the present. This type of historical exegesis is commonly found in the literature of political thought. In other words, much of political theory has been given over to the history of political thought; constant references are still found to the classic writers—Hobbes, Locke, Bentham, Mill, Burke, Machiavelli, Rousseau, Hegel and Hume.

Political scientists have been much concerned with historical literature, and considerable controversy occurs about its value. To Sheldon Wolin:

> In studying the writings of Plato, Locke, or Marx, we are in reality familiarizing ourselves with a fairly stable vocabulary and a set of categories that help orient us towards a particular world, the world of political phenomena. But more than this, since the history of political philosophy is an intellectual development wherein successive thinkers have added new dimensions to the analysis and understanding of politics, an inquiry into that development is not so much a venture into antiquarianism as a form of political education.[2]

Another political thinker who strongly defends the proposition that political philosophy is important for political science is Professor Leo Strauss. He asserts: "Political science requires clarification of what distinguishes political things from things which are not political; it requires that the question be raised and answered 'what is political?' This question cannot be dealt with scientifically but only dialectically."[3]

---

[1] The reader who wishes to master a one-volume history of Western political thought has many choices. Perhaps the classic account is still George H. Sabine, *A History of Political Theory* (New York: Henry Holt, 1950). An extremely well-written account is to be found in Lee C. McDonald, *Western Political Theory* (New York: Harcourt, Brace and World, 1968). A fine non-chronological account is offered by Sheldon Wolin, *Politics and Vision* (Boston: Little, Brown, 1960).

[2] Wolin, *Politics and Vision*, p. 27.

[3] Leo Strauss, *What Is Political Philosophy?* (Glencoe, Ill.: Free Press, 1959), pp. 24-25.

Critics of the historical approach to political thought charge that too much emphasis is placed on reporting what great thinkers have said, with very little attempt at critical analysis of these doctrines. Primary attention is given to the special problems that stimulated a man's ideas and the social context that nourished his thought. Or an attempt may be made to restate or translate the ideas of the great thinkers to manifest their relevance to matters of present concern. Critics feel that political scientists thus give their attention to matters that could better be left to students of history and philosophy. The preoccupation with reporting and restating has exacted too high a price in neglect of the critical evaluation of ideas.

The proposed alternatives to the traditional occupation of political theorists have generally been discussed under the heading of behavioralism or empirical theory. One might note at this point that the arguments between traditional and behavioral political scientists have been conducted in all of the subdisciplines of political science. The behavioral approach has had an uneven penetration in the various fields of political science. Regardless of the field, however, the main controversies involve the degree of scientific objectivity which can be obtained in political analysis and the role of values in political inquiry.

The Problem of Objectivity in Political Analysis

In modern social science usage, the term *science* denotes the systematic, objective study of empirical phenomena and the resultant bodies of knowledge. While most contemporary social scientists would probably concur with this definition of science, the difficulties arise in relation to each of the qualifying adjectives: *systematic, objective,* and *empirical.*

A group of contemporary political scientists have adopted a natural science methodology and call themselves "behavioralists."[4] Broadly speaking, they continue some of the earlier scientific emphases in politics, such as those of Arthur F.

---

[4] For a succinct exposition of behavioral orientations to political inquiry, see Heinz Eulau, *The Behavioral Persuasion in Politics.* (New York: Random House, 1963).

Bentley,[5] Charles E. Merriam,[6] and Graham Wallas.[7] Behavioralists focus not on the forms and legal powers of government but on the politically oriented behavior of individuals and groups. They argue that the reliance on formal deductive methods is often misplaced, and they prefer to invest their intellectual capital in the application of precise methods of analysis to political behavior and the development of rigorous research designs. The behavioralists see political science as coterminous with the other behavioral sciences and view their problems as interdisciplinary in scope. They believe that empirical findings should have a bearing on the development of political theory. Any efforts to approach political data in terms of methodological rigor and the solution of empirical dilemmas can be considered part of the behavioral innovation. The behavioralists are prepared to defend the proposition that political science has claimed its place as a modern social science by concentrating on the empirical investigation of relationships among people. The scientific aim is to establish generalizations about political behavior that are supported by empirical evidence collected in an impersonal and objective way. This evidence must be capable of verification by other scholars and the procedures must be completely open to review and duplication.

As previously noted, behavioral science extends far beyond the boundaries of political science. In many of its aspects, it is a "unity of science" approach in that there are continuities in research problems and terminology. The findings of behavioral scientists in various fields have close relationships with those in other fields. Behavioral science is a combined endeavor of many fields investigating all aspects of behavior, leading to an understanding of human beings as individuals and as elements in social and political groups. Behavioral science therefore includes many studies in such fields as anthropology, economics,

---

[5] See Arthur F. Bentley, *The Process of Government* (Bloomington, Ind.: Principia Press, 1935).

[6] See Charles E. Merriam, *New Aspects of Politics* (Chicago: University of Chicago Press, 1925).

[7] See Graham Wallas, *Human Nature in Politics* (New York: Appleton-Century-Crofts, 1908).

psychology, sociology, psychiatry, linguistics and political science.

The overlapping and duplication of scholarly effort at times borders on chaos. For example, both anthropology and sociology sometimes are claimed to be integrating sciences, the former taking "culture" as the basic idea and the latter focusing on "society." Economics and political science continually inter-relate economic and political behavior, and both employ psychological hypotheses and decision theory. This kind of overlapping indicates that a primary need is to increase the cross-fertilization between the behavioral sciences as presently organized. Common problems and controversies recurring across the fields suggest the benefits of interdisciplinary co-operation.

Behaviorally oriented political scientists have been instrumental in arguing for the goal of maximum scientific objectivity in political analysis. Once this goal is conceded as worth striving for, a number of consequences follow. Problems of experiment and control, of research design, and of operating assumptions become important to the training of political scientists. The scope, objectives, and methods of political science as a discipline assume a number of departures from the traditional orientation of the field. Granted that what is sound in the older methods and approaches can probably be absorbed in the behavioralist approach, the fact remains that there is a distinctive tone to the behavioral persuasion which has stirred bitter arguments among political scientists during the past two decades.

Any attempt to pinpoint the characteristics of behavioralism is arbitrary. David Easton has done as well as anyone in the effort to present the intellectual foundations on which the movement has been constructed. According to Easton, the major tenets of the behavioral credo which distinguish it from the more traditional orientations in political research are:

1. *Regularities*. There are discoverable uniformities in political behavior. These can be expressed in generalizations or theories with explanatory and predictive value.

2. *Verification.* The validity of such generalizations must be able to be tested, in principle, by reference to relevant behavior.
3. *Techniques.* Means for acquiring and interpreting data cannot be taken for granted. They are problematic and need to be examined, refined, and validated so that rigorous means can be found for observing, recording, and analyzing behavior.
4. *Quantification.* Precision in the recording of data and the statement of findings requires measurement and quantification, wherever possible, relevant, and meaningful in the light of other objectives.
5. *Values.* Ethical evaluation and empirical explanation involve two different kinds of propositions that, for the sake of clarity, should be kept analytically distinct. A student of political behavior is not prohibited, however, from asserting propositions of either kind separately or in combination as long as he does not mistake one for the other.
6. *Systematization.* Research ought to be systematic; that is to say, theory and research are to be seen as closely intertwined parts of a coherent and orderly body of knowledge. Research untutored by theory may prove trivial, and theory unsupportable by data, futile.
7. *Pure science.* The application of knowledge is as much a part of the scientific enterprise as theoretical understanding. The understanding and explanation of political behavior logically precedes and provides the basis for efforts to utilize political knowledge in the solution of urgent practical problems of society.
8. *Integration.* Because the social sciences deal with the whole human situation, political research can ignore the findings of other disciplines only at the peril of weakening the validity and undermining the generality of its own results. Recognition of this interrelationship will help to bring political science back to its status of

earlier centuries and return it to the main fold of the social sciences.[8]

Of course, the new political science is hardly a monolithic movement with a universally accepted creed. Its proponents may and do differ over various priorities in the formulation of theory and methodology. They disagree over the utility of various concepts, analytical techniques, and principles of verification. They disagree over assumptions about the nature of man and his functioning in the empirical realm. Every scholar accentuates his own emphases and thereby becomes his own behavioralist. Relative emphases bring different aspects of the landscape into prominence; nevertheless, there are also essential substantive implications. The behavioral approach testifies to the coming of age of theory in the social sciences as a whole, wedded to a commitment to the assumptions and methods of empirical science.

Behavioral science is empirical, rational, general, and cumulative; it is all four at once. Scientific political analysis is distinctive in the systematic attention it gives to the accumulation of objective evidence. For students of political behavior, a problem becomes scientific when it can be formulated in such a way as to test the main proposition asserted about personal or group behavior in a given political situation. The political scientist attempts to formulate a hypothesis to explain the phenomena he is observing. A hypothesis is a proposed answer or solution to a problem which is assumed (perhaps without belief) for the purpose of exploring and expanding the logical consequences of the assumed answer or solution.

The role of hypotheses in scientific research is to suggest explanations for certain facts and to guide in the investigation of others. We cannot take a single step forward in any inquiry unless we begin with a suggested explanation or solution of the

---

[8] David Easton, "The Current Meaning of 'Behavioralism' in Political Science," in James C. Charlesworth, editor, *The Limits of Behavioralism in Political Science* (Philadelphia: American Academy of Political and Social Science, 1962), pp. 7-8.

difficulty which originated it. The two basic rules of a good hypothesis are that it answer the problem and that it be testable, either directly or indirectly. A well formulated hypothesis leads the scientist to just those facts which are relevant. The function of an hypothesis is to direct our search for the order among the observed facts.

Hypotheses may be developed from various sources. An hypothesis may be based simply on an informed guess or idea, or it may stem from a body of theory that leads to a prediction that if certain conditions are present, certain results will follow. Regardless of their origin, hypotheses are tentative explanations suggested to us by something in the subject matter and by our previous knowledge. In constructing hypotheses we have to go beyond the facts at hand: the hypothetical objects are at first conjured up by a disciplined creative imagination. Probably no rules can be given for this kind of conjuring. We do know that the greatest thinkers are not the men who made new observations or drew logical conclusions from given axioms but those geniuses who made new and unexpected guesses about hypothetical objects. We noted earlier that the great thinker is not a mere collector of facts; he is more like a creative artist who gives us a new and unexpected insight into the nature of things.

The formulation of hypotheses varies with the nature of the problem and the extent of our prior knowledge about it. Formulation and reformulation of research questions is a continuing process. Observation does not bear fruit unless questions have previously been defined. As far as possible these questions ought to take the form of working hypotheses; that is, an answer is postulated at the same time as the question. The aim of the subsequent research effort is to find out whether this answer is correct.

The hypotheses employed in inquiry are bound to the facts that are found; the assumed facts influence the further development of hypotheses by linking the conceptual and the empirical.[9] There is a constant interplay between empirical data and

---

[9] Rollo Handy, *Methodology of the Behavioral Sciences: Problems and Controversies* (Springfield, Ill.: Charles C. Thomas, 1964), p. 169.

imaginative reasoning. When Alfred North Whitehead was asked: "Which are more important, facts or ideas?" the great philosopher reflected briefly and replied: "Ideas about facts." This intricate relationship between theory and empirical inquiry is basic to scientific political analysis. The worlds of empirical data and theoretical constructs are complementary for the student of comparative politics. Brute facts are rendered intelligible by reason, and reason draws its sustenance from experience. Reason without experience is empty, and experience without reason is blind. Behavioralists want to accumulate empirical data in order to facilitate the testing of hypotheses about political behavior.

Those who are critical of the behavioral approach in its quest for maximum scientific objectivity in political analysis maintain that the underlying methodology of the natural sciences is inapplicable to political study. They suggest that the behavioralists are pursuing a phantom objectivity that has never existed and never will. Objectivity is far more difficult to achieve in all of the social sciences than in any of the natural sciences because the social scientist is a member of society, occupying a particular position in it. His position is from within the system that he seeks to observe from outside, that is, objectively.

The scientific study of society is enormously difficult because men inevitably bring to their study of society a body of ideas and preconceptions that may affect their observations and bias their conclusions. Whereas the natural scientist deals with phenomena which are essentially independent of human volition, the social scientist is involved with the behavior of human beings who cannot be manipulated like material objects. The phenomena that political science investigates are distinctly human, involving purpose, change, and evaluation.

In addition, political science must deal with collective entities such as groups and institutions that cannot be described or explained solely in terms of individual behavior. The most distinctive work of the behavioral approach so far has dealt with individuals who vote, take part in politics, or express certain attitudes or beliefs. But an individual is not a political system, and analysis of such individual preferences cannot fully explain collective decisions; yet the classic concern of students of politics with the analysis of systems of individuals and groups will obviously continue to be explored. It is therefore argued that all explanation of political events is likely to remain partial and nonpredictive.

From an initial, if oversimplified perspective, one can say that the difference between the approach of the natural and the social sciences is that the former is "objective" and the latter is "subjective."[10] The social scientist looks at society from the inside, much as if one had asked Jonah to study the anatomy of the whale. Seeing it from such a point of view introduces a perspective that may distort what is observed. There are intrinsic difficulties to impartial observation which must be guarded against constantly by the student of social and political phenomena. We have to remind ourselves that the demand for objectivity is the demand for an abstract and unrealizable situation in which the observer is an unobtrusive, passive, and passionless machine who records without discrimination whatever comes before him. Since every human observer is subject to various lapses of discrimination in his observations, some inanimate machine is clearly more appropriate for the attainment of such "objectivity." Unfortunately, such a machine, if devised, would be incapable of yielding much insight into human behavior. The data which it recorded so meticulously would still have to be interpreted by human intelligence to attain relevance and meaning for the human condition. Cyberneticians say that even their most advanced computers have only a minute proportion of the operational efficiency of the brain of a not very well endowed or well trained human being. All of our immensely sophisticated social science techniques are

---

[10] For an account of this argument in more detail than can be given here, see F. A. Hayek, *The Counter-Revolution of Science: Studies in the Abuse of Reason* (Glencoe, Ill.: Free Press, 1952).

still crude in comparison with the complexity of what the average man feels every day of the week.

The behavioralist might reply at this point that much of the training of a political scientist is (or ought to be) training that will enable the investigator to transcend his personal views and prejudices in order to examine the situation "as it is." He can wear corrective lenses, as it were, so as to reduce the subjective influences to a considerable extent and to guard his observations from their distorting effect.

There may be much validity in this solution. Nevertheless, the political scientist is not a man from Mars; he cannot escape his humanity. Even with the best of intentions and the most sophisticated methodological tools, the political scientist is still a product of his heredity and environment, his temperament and his emotions, his own convictions and preferences. Some biases may be an ingrained part of his intellectual machinery; they can exert their influence on his judgment and reactions even when he is least conscious of them. Moreover, some of the worst biases are not those that are private to a few social scientists but those shared by the whole community of social scientists. The latter kind of bias has the insidious effect of appearing to be "objective" because it is a communal assumption. When this occurs, the entire universe of discourse of a group of cooperating scientists is infected.

There is general agreement among social scientists that *empirical* phenomena are phenomena that can be observed by trained scientific observers, but there has been continual disagreement about whether or not it is necessary to deal with phenomena that cannot be directly so observed. Some have asserted that *only* phenomena which can be directly observed should be conceptualized in the social sciences. Against this assertion has been placed the tradition that the central variables of the social sciences are frequently "subjective" variables such as value and motive. We can see this disagreement exemplified in much of the literature of the social sciences, some writers stressing the "objective" variables while others grapple with the "subjective" variables.

Critics of the behavioralists argue that attempting to make the social sciences too much like the natural sciences would blind the social scientist to the "subjective" variables, which are often crucial elements of the situation under analysis. Put in other words, critics of the behavioralists fear that the reduction of political phenomena to nothing but measurable quantity distorts and oversimplifies the complexity of political reality, simply because so many critically important aspects of political life cannot be isolated in this fashion.

Professor Hayek comments on this problem by saying: "Most of the objects of social or human action are not 'objective facts' in the special narrow sense in which this term is used by the Sciences . . . and they cannot at all be defined in physical terms."[11] The data of the social sciences are abstractions from all the physical attributes of the things in question; their definitions are elaborated entirely in terms of the mental attitudes of men toward those things. The facts of political and social life cannot be deduced from the brute facts of the biological life of the individuals composing the society. Other levels of analysis are required for a rounded investigation of human behavior.

There would, perhaps, be little objection to the behavioral approach if it simply reported and attempted to generalize about quantifiable elements of political phenomena. Most behavioralists purport to establish a universally applicable political science in which the quantifiable is all that is "scientifically" analyzable. Critics of behavioralism maintain that a sufficiently sensitive scientific method should be free from the illusion that nothing is "scientific" unless it is reduced to the laws of mathematical formulae. They further argue that there is little reason to believe that mathematical approaches will produce a consensus among political scientists. Access to computers and proficiency in the calculus does not transform a mediocre mind into a superior intellect. Mathematical political scientists have no greater perception of reality than their nonquantitatively oriented brethren. Political scientists must still pay attention to

---

[11] Ibid., pp. 26-27.

those aspects of political life not readily amenable to statistical counting and correlation. The results of such inquiry may be impressionistic at times but there is also a closer sense of human reality. Robert Dahl, who has championed behavioral and empirical approaches in his writing, has remarked that "empirical political science had better find a place for speculation."[12] This observation is well grounded in historical perspective, for speculation has very frequently preceded great advance in scientific theory.

In this discussion we have raised some rather far-reaching philosophical issues which can hardly be resolved here in any definitive fashion. Science, both as knowledge and as method, incorporates rational and empirical elements in its pursuit of reliable knowledge.[13] Intuition and speculation need not be excluded from scientific inquiry but must, in fact, be incorporated as part of a process in which such insights are subject to systematic testing by a relevant frame of reference. What distinguishes the social sciences from each other are the procedures and emphases of each discipline. There is overlapping at many points, nor is any intellectual scandal involved in this state of affairs; the natural sciences are in the same situation.

We are faced with awkward and serious difficulties in our efforts at objective observation of human affairs. Even under the most favorable conditions, our senses are not always able to provide us with objective knowledge about what we set out to observe. Sometimes social scientists are reluctant to admit that observation is not always neutral in its effects. Observation may influence what is being observed and possibly does not record what would have occurred had there been no observation, yet, modern science is unquestionably rooted in observation, whether at firsthand or whether derived from the observations of other investigators. It is necessary to recognize quite frankly the obstacles to impartial observation. Our sense organs

---

[12] Robert A. Dahl, "The Behavioral Approach in Political Science: Epitaph for a Monument to a Successful Protest," *American Political Science Review*, vol. 55 (December 1961), p. 772.

[13] Ibid.

operate in a highly variable, erratic, and selective manner; the notion that they act like machines, conveying to us the sensations produced by external stimuli, is an untenable pretense. Eyewitnesses are notoriously unreliable. What we observe is only a selective ordering of the total reality which is there for us to observe. As psychologists have clearly demonstrated, men often see what they wish to see because of the preconceptions they have acquired in constructing a frame of reference through the years.

The only honest way that one can respond to this difficulty is to do his utmost to objectify observations. There are, surely, degrees of objectivity among students of society: some observers are more objective than others. Systematic training in the nature and methods of political inquiry potentially make it possible to control one's biases by becoming aware of them. One can also master the various techniques of observation which are designed to serve as tools of scientific inquiry. Observation, in fact, is a research technique which should be purposefully integrated with other steps in the research process.[14] The observation of everyday life is haphazard, but scientific techniques and specific training can lead toward that goal of accurate analysis of social phenomena. Social scientists can, and often do, achieve a remarkable degree of objectivity, and we certainly need not despair of the efforts to achieve this desired goal.

The notion that there is only one method to achieve knowledge of an overall view of human experience is a form of mental colorblindness. It does seem apparent that the behavioral sciences are not scientific in the sense that the physical and biological sciences are scientific. Must we therefore conclude that knowledge of a substantive nature, even if not strictly scientific, fails to be a fertile source of significant questions, insights, concepts, ideals, and empirical data? Merely to know

---

[14] For a richly illustrated account on specific aspects of research methods, see Claire Sellitz, Marie Jahoda, Morton Deutsch, and Stuart W. Cook, *Research Methods in Social Relations* (New York: Holt, Rinehart and Winston, 1959).

politics in an empirical way is insufficient. In all social sciences, events and ideas are mixed to a degree, but in political science the link is especially close and crucial to inquiry.[15]

Objectivity has to do with attitudes and practices that are generally accepted within the profession regarding the criteria by which data are judged to be relevant and reliable. Professional objectivity appears primarily as a personal quality of the researcher which makes him concerned about rational, dispassionate analysis of the subject at hand. The scholar may be interested in his research, but he will not allow himself to be swayed by his personal prejudices and preferences in the conduct of his inquiry. In the formulation of Carl J. Friedrich, the political scientist must strive for "a special kind of objectivity which understands its own subjectivity and transcends it."[16]

The Status of Values in Political Analysis

Concern with values is at the core of all political theory. A political system is an enactment of values and ideas which form an integrated whole. The relationship between values is at the very heart of all political phenomena. In recent years, the value orientation of political and social inquiry has been receiving increasing recognition. This orientation has had to contend with the opposing viewpoint which argues that the social sciences should be value free, in the sense that the value commitments of the social scientist should play no role in his analysis of social and political data. We shall now examine the dispute concerning values as objects of inquiry on the one hand and as personal commitments on the other hand.

Values as Objects of Inquiry

In 1917, the German sociologist, Max Weber, published an essay entitled "The Meaning of 'Ethical Neutrality' in Soci-

---

[15] For a thoughtful essay in support of this view, see Neal Wood, "Political Behavioralism," *Commonweal* (October 4, 1968), pp. 17-22. Professor Wood, a Canadian political theorist, asserts that behavioralists have failed to clarify the conception of "objectivity."

[16] Carl J. Friedrich, *Man and His Government: An Empirical Theory of Politics* (New York: McGraw-Hill, 1963), p. 44.

ology and Economics."[17] In this important analysis of the implications of a value-free social science, Weber proposed a kind of self-discipline aimed at "ethical neutrality" as a goal of the student of society. His analysis was largely provoked by opposition to the German professors who were using their academic posts to bring political influence to bear on their students in the classroom. To counter them, Weber advocated that the value commitments of the social scientist should play no role in his analysis of social data.

Weber did not want the academic lecture hall turned into a political arena or a religious pulpit. He believed that the ultimate value commitments of each social scientist would determine the problems in which he was interested and the range of data he would investigate. To Weber, academic knowledge would never enable us to interpret the meaning of the world; at best, it can only force us to clarify the modes of commitment which underlie our own particular interpretations. Such interpretations, in Weber's view, are essentially arbitrary: evaluative standpoints are immune to argument. In other words, Weber maintained that one cannot leap from an "is" to an "ought." A political philosophy is like a taste for beer: one can only state one's brand and go away—there is no point in arguing the merits of such subjective tastes. Thus, Weber's world is one in which there are as many different social sciences as there are modes of ultimate commitment. For example, no amount of historical research is going to make a Catholic and a Freemason agree in their interpretation of religious history (although even Weber conceded that some discussion might be useful and might oblige one of the parties to modify his position).

This concession did not imply any modification of Weber's basic dichotomy between fact and value. Descriptive statements, being factual, assert alleged truths about reality. They deal with what is, not with what ought to be. Normative statements express conceptions of the desirable. They indicate value prefer-

---

[17] See E. A. Shils and H. A. Finch, editors, *Max Weber on the Methodology of the Social Sciences* (Glencoe, Ill.: The Free Press, 1949), pp. 1-47.

ences and often endorse purposes or norms. Weber saw no way of establishing what ought to be by observing what does exist in reality. He could see no way of verifying normative statements by using empirical methods, no logical way of proceeding from the realm of fact to the realm of value.[18]

However, having said this, one should not fail to point out that Weber regarded such strict ethical neutrality as an unattainable ideal which should nevertheless be attempted: "The possible is often reached only by striving to attain the impossible that lies beyond it."[19] Weber recognized that the social scientist could not escape the problem of values and had to grapple with them in theoretical schemes and ideal type models that he might construct and elaborate. The social scientist must examine values in order to assess their implications and internal coherence in terms of socially formulated goals.

Max Weber was convinced that sociology required a precise formulation as a scientific discipline. The unit of analysis, once determined, is subject to genuine scientific study by the same methods in all science. Weber's actual procedure consisted primarily in the construction of typologies of behavior and comparative analysis conducted on the basis of such typologies. Many of the significant trends in contemporary social science are continuations of the work begun by him. Among these are the study of bureaucracy, the sociology of law, the sociology of politics, and the study of charismatic leadership. Weber also pioneered in the study of authority. Scholars who have followed in the footsteps of Weber have continued the effort to prevent values from influencing the conduct and the results of social inquiry.

Political scientists who are dedicated to the use of scientific method do not all line up in opposition to the study of values. Many who are in the behavioral wing of the profession maintain that values ought to be examined scientifically. Value analysis and the description of value systems can be achieved

---

[18] Ibid., p. 83.
[19] Ibid., p. 24.

by scientific study. Dependable, trustworthy statements about values as ends can be supplied by study which meets the tests of scientific method. The scholar can make searching inquiries into how different values have actually been formed and brought into balance by competing social forces. He can analyze how the structures of associated values are altered over time and how particular values rise and fall in the evolution of men and nations. The regime of competing values offers enough material to occupy a scholar for a lifetime.

There is no logical inconsistency in maintaining that while values are a legitimate object of study, the social scientist has no justification for intruding his own assessment of the relative worth of alternative value systems. But there are practical grounds for doubting whether any human being is capable of the kind of detachment required of the true neutral. This doubt exists simply because values affect the choice of facts and the manner of evaluating them. Values may flow into investigations of political behavior at almost any stage of the research process, from initial selection of the problems to the final interpretation of findings.

Like it or not, values are part and parcel of the political world we want to investigate. The hardest problems confronting scholars and citizens are very frequently problems of conflicting values. By their choices and behavior, people strive to attain what they perceive as worthwhile in life and reject what they regard as unworthy. These affirmations of worth always cost something in terms of the allocation of scarce resources, efforts exerted, and time invested in attempting to attain them. In practice, values are often not subjective ideals but are empirical sources of conflict which involve concrete gains and losses.

Scales of values are variously held at different times by different groups and societies. Each individual person or group wants to follow its own value pattern and regards its own norms as the best guide to happiness. Such are the data with which politics must work. The very life and movement of a society rests on a structure of values which must be sustained and promoted if the community is to survive. Were it not for values and the associated attitudes and beliefs which accompany them, people would feel lost in their environment. They would be disoriented in their relations with social and physical objects. They would lack a basis upon which to respond to their environment.[20] The bases of community and consensus would be seriously eroded in the absence of the cohesive structure of an integrated value system.

Values, considered as objects of inquiry, are therefore facts, given as much as any other facts. Norms and values, whether ideal or operative, are crucial items on the agenda of political inquiry. *Value* is a particular dimension of being: namely, the dimension of "ought to be." Values change, like everything else, but in changing they continue to be objectified.

Although the political scientist attempts to make his initial observations of political phenomena as factual and objective as possible, he finds it difficult to adhere strictly to this ideal. The student can test this assertion for himself simply by turning to the literature of political science. Despite frequent protestations to the contrary, this body of research findings is permeated with value judgments. The political scientist does not have immunity from biases of many kinds. Full objectivity is an ideal toward which we are constantly striving but which we never attain in its pristine purity. For all his efforts, the political scientist never succeeds in liberating himself entirely from dependence on the dominant preconceptions of his environment.

Such value distortion cannot be completely eliminated by any combination of research methods. Political science deals with data that are especially value laden, because political phenomena almost invariably have implications for the observer's preferences. Furthermore, political science has developed a tradition of deliberately normative theorizing; many political theorists intentionally focus on value-laden propositions. Theory in the study of politics has been commonly used

---

[20] Lewis A. Froman, Jr., *People and Politics: An Analysis of the American Political System* (Englewood Cliffs, N. J.: Prentice-Hall, 1962), pp. 21-22.

to stipulate ideals and set standards by which to judge political action.[21]

One of the best indications for the successful development of a more mature social science in our society is the increasing awareness among political scientists of the nature of the scientific task which confronts them in regard to the treatment of values. All of the social science disciplines have deep roots in the positivistic bias of a great deal of nineteenth-century social theory; even now they have not entirely cast off the influence of this misconceived and limited understanding of human behavior.[22] There are still positivistic social scientists who either ignore or deny the whole area of the moral and emotional dimensions of human existence and who try to understand all of human activity in terms of man's rational orientation to the world. But, as we have argued in this section, not all that is nonempirical is "unreal." There is no inevitable conflict between the social sciences and the humanities: each of these is a necessary discipline in man's understanding of his social existence. They are complementary spheres of interest, the social sciences striving to develop systematic understandings of human behavior and the humanistic studies providing those insights which anticipate the future progress of the social sciences.

The political scientist, so far as he is a scientist, must adhere to the canons of his discipline. But no man is a scientist all of the time; the moral or ethical neutrality appropriate to scientific inquiry does not extend to all areas of life. The political scientist lives in a community and has personal values which he shares in greater or lesser degree with his colleagues and fellow citizens. Human behavior and human aspirations are both worthy of continual consideration from students of society

---

[21] See David G. Smith, "Political Science and Political Theory," *American Political Science Review* (September 1957).

[22] For a critique of the positivist social science view, see Hans J. Morgenthau, *Scientific Man vs. Power Politics* (Chicago: University of Chicago Press, 1946).

in their attempt to capture the essential core of what Bernard Barber calls "the Order of Human Nature."[23]

Political analysis is infused with value. The problem for methodology is not *whether* values are involved in an inquiry, but *which,* and above all, *how* they are to be incorporated into the scientific enterprise. Values are always relevant and, sometimes, crucial for the study of political phenomena. Rational thought is applied to both empirical and nonempirical data. As science has advanced steadily into areas that were formerly considered nonempirical, some of us have apparently assumed that eventually only science would remain so that there would be no nonempirical problems left. Yet science itself depends upon certain ultimate, nonempirical social values and worldviews. The extreme positivist position that science is all sufficient for human adjustment has come to seem untenable even to many who formerly held it. There have been important developments in recent social science which assert the contrary position.[24]

The newer approach maintains that the nonempirical entities referred to by social values, religious ideas, and other ideologies have necessary and independent status. Although such entities are, of course, affected by scientific ideas, they have a measure of autonomy and are not wholly reducible to empirical science proper. This being so, science alone can never provide a complete adjustment to the natural and social world for man. Life without values has no meaning, and science can contribute only indirectly to the creation of values. Man can live without science, technology, or political scientists but the absence of values makes society impossible. In the final analysis, this is the chief reason why the omnipotence of science in hu-

---

[23] Bernard Barber, *Science and the Social Order* (Glencoe, Ill.: Free Press, 1952), p. 262.

[24] For illustrations of this position, see David Easton, *The Political System* (New York: Knopf, 1953); Friedrich, *Man and His Government;* C. Wright Mills, *The Sociological Imagination* (New York: Oxford University Press, 1959); and Meehan, *The Theory and Method of Political Analysis.*

man life is impossible and undesirable. As Michael Curtis has said: "A value-free social science is appropriate for computers, not for men. For the student of comparative politics, a sense of irony may be as useful as a computer. . . ."[25]

No political analysis has ever been undertaken without touching on values. Most political scientists believe that at least some kinds of value questions are proper for professional consideration. The problem, then, becomes a matter of how values should be treated in political inquiry. We have seen that a scholar can focus his research efforts on the factual political system to the exclusion of the way it ought to be. This was Max Weber's prescription for social research, and this approach is still assumed by many contemporary political scientists.[26]

Few subjects have received more polemical attention than the issue of values in political analysis, and the controversy has not entirely faded away.[27] Values have been discussed from so many different viewpoints that the dialogue is often obscured by verbal confusion. Some of the major controversies about the problem of values as objects of inquiry can hardly be discussed sensibly unless there is agreement as to the use of the term. The term *values* has been used in numerous ways, both in philosophy and the various sciences. Sociologically, *values* may be defined as those criteria according to which the individual or society judges the importance of persons, patterns, goals, and other sociocultural objects. Values, therefore, are the criteria that give meaning and significance to the total culture and society. More fully described, the values of concern to the social scientist are shared by a plurality of people in the political

---

[25] Michael Curtis, *Comparative Government and Politics*, 2d ed. (New York: Harper and Row, 1978), p. 13.

[26] For a closely reasoned and stimulating defense of "scientific value relativism," see Arnold Brecht, *Political Theory: The Foundations of Twentieth Century Political Thought* (Princeton: Princeton University Press, 1959).

[27] Perhaps the most passionate attack on value-free research attempts can be found in the writing of Leo Strauss. See, for example, *Natural Right and History* (Chicago: University of Chicago Press, 1953). Equally opposed to such approaches is Eric Voegelin, *The New Science of Politics* (Chicago: University of Chicago Press, 1952).

system. They are viewed as necessary for the preservation of the common welfare. Values involve emotions; people may be moved to sacrifice for the maintenance of the highest values. For this reason, values are closely related to patterns of political behavior and the operation of the political process.

Values may be classified most meaningfully according to their institutional function in the culture. It is quite common to identify and discuss separately values that are religious, political, economic, and so forth. There is a set of values employed in each of the major institutions of a society. The mere presence of values brings about certain political and social consequences.

It is possible to examine values as observable facts associated with human activity. The values people hold and their consequences for social action are social facts in the same sense as any other part of their activities. In considering this, there are clearly two factions within the social science disciplines. One faction enthusiastically embraces the scientific ideal that envisions the possibility of a social science anchored in a rigorous and systematic empiricism; it observes more closely, records more precisely, and employs more sophisticated concepts and tools of analysis than social science has in the past.[28] The other faction asserts that counting and measuring are sometimes substitutes for thought. The notion of universal and invariant relationships, founded on a science of human behavior, must yield to a much less rigorous conception of the nature of political and social inquiry.[29] The search for scientific precision must be moderated in the face of the complexities of human societies and the human condition. The attempt to predict countless individual human acts must be renounced as a goal of social science inquiry.

Regardless of how one answers the questions posed in the

---

[28] For a comprehensive presentation of the problems involved in striving for such systematic inquiry, see Abraham Kaplan, *The Conduct of Inquiry: Methodology for Behavioral Science* (San Francisco: Chandler Pub. Co., 1964).

[29] For a brilliant justification of this position see Michael Polanyi, *Personal Knowledge* (Chicago: University of Chicago Press, 1958).

previous discussion, men and women do have values (whether they are conscious of all of them or not). The scholar's personal participation in his research efforts is an indispensable part of science itself. We shall now examine some of the questions which arise from this unavoidable reality.

Values as Personal Preferences and Commitments

In our previous discussion of objectivity, we noted that human sense organs are unreliable and selective in their reaction to various external stimuli. A similar statement can be made with regard to the observer's value system. One of the contributions of Karl Marx to social science was to point out how a man's social class and economic status tend to influence his attitudes, determine his assumptions, and distort his judgments without his being aware of it. Reality alters with the value-laden eye of the beholder. The descriptions made are dependent on the perspective of the particular observer. Marx himself gives us a highly selective version of reality by portraying a single type of conditioning factor, the economic, as all important. Facts about living things are more highly personal than the facts of the inanimate world.[30] Values differ from one culture to another, and men's ideas are greatly influenced by their backgrounds and value preconceptions. Most generalizations in political science research are limited to a particular culture. Much of social science is culture-bound, structured within the limits of a particular cultural situation.

One way to react to this state of affairs is simply to embrace it and live cheerfully with it. Thus George Kateb concludes: "the description of political deeds and policies is inherently ambiguous . . . the language of political science is loaded . . . and cannot be cleansed without becoming senseless. This is the natural condition of political studies, and those in search of scientific precision had better expend their labors in the sciences."[31] Professor Kateb is not convinced that the

---

30 Ibid. p. 347.
31 George Kateb, *Political Theory: Its Nature and Uses* (New York: St. Martin's Press, 1968), p. 84.

quest for hypotheses is a rewarding activity for political studies; he regards this approach to politics as too constrictive for the political imagination to exercise its sensibilities.

A similar position is advanced by David G. Smith. He states: "Political theory, in its most constructive and ambitious endeavors, is literary in form. . . . Like the novelist, the political theorist paints pictures in words of a political life that we might choose, or that we are now leading but do not fully comprehend. He records his reflections upon politics to help us to decide how we are to live."[32] Smith flatly denies that political science is a behavioral science concerned with general laws. Rather, he maintains that the subject matter of political science is basically the specific problem and the particular institution. Smith concludes: "Casting the language of politics in the rigorous formulae of a given scientific framework may produce logical order; but it will also achieve disciplined and persistent perversity in the discussion of moral and democratic issues."[33]

We obviously cannot shed our values the way we remove our coats. Values are an integral part of the human personality; we can assume that these preferences and attitudes will always be with us. The political scientist who claims utter impartiality and neutrality has simply driven his moral views so far underground that he is no longer aware of them. There is overwhelming evidence to indicate that the impact upon research of one's moral outlook is both wide and varied. One of the first thinkers to analyze this reciprocal relationship was the German sociologist, Karl Mannheim.[34]

The particular values of a given individual will depend upon the culture and various subcultures into which he was socialized and upon incidents and accidents of his personal experiences. Values provide the framework which shapes the selection of empirical problems for investigation and influences the interpretation of the data. Our very ability to perceive re-

---

[32] Smith, "Political Science," p. 746.

[33] Ibid., p. 740.

[34] Karl Mannheim, *Ideology and Utopia* (New York: Harcourt, Brace, 1949).

lations among facts often depends upon the insights gained from immersion in a particular moral outlook.

Since values are inescapably present, each analyst must come to terms with them in his work. The distinguished Swedish political economist, Gunnar Myrdal, has these observations on the value situation in social science research:

> We employ and we need value premises in making scientific observations of facts and in analyzing their causal interrelation. Chaos does not organize itself into cosmos. We need viewpoints and they presume valuations. A "disinterested social science" is, from this viewpoint, pure nonsense. It never existed, and it will never exist. We can strive to make our thinking rational in spite of this, but only by facing the valuations, not by evading them.[35]

Myrdal believes that when valuations are driven underground they hinder observation and inference from becoming truly objective. He maintains that this kind of avoidance can be overcome only by making the valuations explicit. Since valuations cannot be excluded from scientific analysis, Myrdal argues they should be self-consciously included: "There is no other device for excluding biases in the social sciences than to face the valuations and to introduce them as explicitly stated, specific, and sufficiently concretized, value premises."[36] Myrdal concludes that the method of working with explicit value premises has an advantage in attempts to lay a rational foundation for social science research. It is better to have the value premises on the table rather than under it. At the very least, this approach indicates that the student has tried to avoid hidden valuations which might otherwise go unremarked if the effort to detect them were not attempted.

We saw in our earlier discussion of methodological choices that one does not escape valuations by restricting research to the discovery of "facts." The very attempt to avoid valuations by doing "value-free" research involves in itself a valuation. Verbally, research may carefully avoid any mention of values,

35 Gunnar Myrdal, *Value in Social Theory* (London: Routledge and Kegan Paul, 1958), p. 54.

36 Ibid., p. 132.

but this in itself is no evidence of their absence. No factual proposition uttered by a human being can be devoid of all relevance to moral preconceptions. When we describe a factual situation, our propositions inevitably flow from some moral purpose that has led us to investigate these facts.[37]

No one begins study with a blank mind. Each social scientist brings to his inquiry a bundle of suppositions, convictions, and beliefs which constitute the major determinants of his judgment regarding what to study and how to go about studying it. According to Charles Hyneman, the scholar marks his product in three ways which involve the injection of personality: by assumptions of risk; by presumptions of knowledge; and by incorporation of value preferences.[38] Science itself presupposes certain values. The moral values of the scholar help determine what he regards as significant for serious study. No one scholar carries quite the same intellectual equipment as any other.

Moral values cannot be factored out of political inquiry if only because the very function of politics is to formulate imperatives and to back them with the force of consensus from the community. We can study social reality from the viewpoint of human ideals. The value connotation of our concepts gives significance to our inquiry; it poses those questions without which there can be no answers. Value premises should not be chosen arbitrarily; they are relevant and significant to the society in which we live. The unity of a culture consists in the fact that to a relatively large degree there exists a certain community of valuations. We should reflect upon the fact that the social sciences have received their impetus more from the urge to improve society than from a clinical curiosity about its working.[39]

Values are prior to any investigation, whether in politics or in any other area of intellectual inquiry. Social science research rests upon a triad of methods, theories, and values. No

---

[37] Easton, *The Political System*, p. 224.
[38] Charles S. Hyneman, *The Study of Politics* (Urbana: University of Illinois Press, 1959), p. 186.
[39] Myrdal, *Value in Social Theory*, p. 9.

problem can be adequately formulated unless the values involved are clarified and conceptualized with careful consideration. Much of the confusion in the social sciences concerns controversy about the nature of science. There is more than a little ambiguity involved in using the term with reference to the study of society. Scientific empiricism means many things, and there is no one accepted version of the criteria implicit in this approach to political and social phenomena.

If we insist on making political analysis as objective as possible, we are inevitably going to seize upon mathematics as the method, *par excellence,* to attempt to attain this objectivity. The rigorous use of mathematical methods and models provides us with incontestable results and forces people to accept our findings as conclusive. The mathematization of the social sciences would culminate in the axiomatic formulation of its contents. The axiomatic method consists of formulating a set of propositions which must be free of contradictions, and the deductions derived from them must contain our knowledge of the field. The axioms will be statements about political behavior in the political system.[40]

It would seem logical that those social scientists who want to escape from the subjectivity of their discipline will increasingly employ mathematical formulae based on quantitative observations of empirical phenomena. Jacques Ellul has stated that the moment the mathematical method is put into operation everything becomes object. We are interested in achieving only that knowledge which can be quantified. According to Ellul:

> When it is a question of man and his society, his state, his law, and his history, can I treat them simply as objects? Can I objectify them so completely that they are no longer anything to me and I am no longer in them? . . . Is there not from the outset some illusion in believing this to be possible? Am I such a stranger to my nation and my class that I can study them with a serenity and

---

[40] For a symposium on the general topic, see James C. Charlesworth, editor, *Mathematics and the Social Sciences: The Utility and Inutility of Mathematics in the Study of Economics, Political Science, and Sociology* (Philadelphia: American Academy of Political and Social Science, 1963).

objectivity that not only disassociate me from them, but reduce them to a dismal state in which everything is possible now that nothing is real? . . . The moment this decision is made . . . the way is open for everything to be *treated* as an object.[41]

Ellul believes that the mathematical method cannot be employed in all instances. Areas exist which are totally irreducible to quantitative terms because they are dependent on qualitative factors which defy measurement.[42] Attempting to reduce these areas to mathematical formulations covers only their outward forms and can lead to serious distortions. Everything that has to do with man is divided into numerical and nonnumerical, with the second part eliminated or ignored in order that the mathematical method may be employed. One must proceed, in other words, "as if" the nonnumerical did not exist so that the numerical can. Once it is admitted that there is a constant relationship between the two dimensions, what appears to be reducible to numbers ceases in reality to be so.[43] Moreover, if one reverses the "as if" proposition to read: "What if the quantitative can be explained only in relation to the qualitative?," then everything that has been arrived at by the application of the mathematical model becomes false.[44]

Ellul raises a final ominous point regarding the potential use of mathematics in social science research. He writes: "If in the name of knowledge you treat the object of cognition with pure objectivity—that is, without love—you will, in the action that follows knowledge, also treat without love this object that you have robbed of its individuality by reducing it to a number."[45] Ellul asserts that the desire to apply mathematics to the study of man in society is the result of a craving for cer-

---

[41] See Jacques Ellul, *A Critique of the New Commonplaces* (New York: Knopf, 1968), pp. 244-45. Ellul strongly denies the proposition that "all science is numerical." He believes that the prestige of the number has a magic aura about it in the scientific community which renders it immune from rational criticism.

[42] Ibid., p. 246.

[43] Ibid., p. 247.

[44] Ibid., p. 248.

[45] Ibid., p. 246.

tainty and perfect knowledge; mathematics thus becomes a substitute for metaphysics, and modern man may find in mathematics the certainty formerly reserved for revelation.[46]

These are rather harsh words. Can Ellul's strictures be refuted by arguments in favor of quantification in the social sciences? As is so frequently the case, there are no formal rules for estimating the utility of mathematics as a tool of political inquiry. The evaluation of this approach will depend heavily on the judgment and experience of the individual social scientist. It would be impossible adequately to cover the various arguments involved in this controversy within the confines of this book. The interested student may wish to explore some of the literature cited in the footnotes of this chapter.[47] However, a few remarks on the implications of mathematics for the study of politics will now be put forth with no pretension of being a comprehensive summary of the issues involved.

With regard to the quantitative-qualitative dichotomy, the distinction is not terribly useful. Aristotle stated that the nature of the subject matter will determine the amount of precision that can be attained in its study. We might paraphrase this advice in the context of this discussion and say that the purpose of the inquiry is the prime determinant of the value of any mathematical approach. Measurement is never an end in itself; it serves certain ends and performs certain functions as an instrumentality to achieve certain specified purposes. It is the failure to accept this rather unexceptional statement that has led some social scientists to seek quantification at all costs, even at the cost of scientific relevance. There is a fruitless straining after the use of mathematics which can only be explained by the

---

[46] Ibid., p. 249.

[47] See Herbert A. Simon, *Models of Man: Social and Rational* (New York: Wiley, 1957); Kenneth J. Arrow, Samuel Karlin, and Patrick Suppes, *Mathematical Methods in the Social Sciences* (Stanford: Stanford University Press, 1960); John G. Kemeny and J. Laurie Snell, *Mathematical Models in the Social Sciences* (Boston: Ginn, 1962); Paul Lazarsfeld, editor, *Mathematical Thinking in the Social Sciences* (Glencoe, Ill.: Free Press, 1954); James S. Coleman, *Introduction to Mathematical Sociology* (Glencoe, Ill.: Free Press, 1964).

higher prestige which the mathematical forms of the physical sciences have for many social scientists.

Mathematics is sometimes called "the only true science." But although mathematics is closely allied with science, it is not substantive science at all. It is, rather, a language of the relations among concepts. This precise and extremely useful language has made possible great advances in many areas of science. But it must never be forgotten that quantification is merely one method of observing, recording, and manipulating data; it is only one way of expressing degrees of qualities and relationships. It is an extremely useful tool for science, but it is not to be confused with the conceptual schemes of science.

In political science, mathematics has proved to be useful for the ordering and analysis of some data, for the development of theory, and for suggesting patterns of theory development by analogy.[48] But the use of mathematics is not the only sign of the existence of a highly developed science. Despite its relative lack of metrical precision, for instance, biology is a respected science with a great range of usefulness. Few would look upon the discipline with disdain simply because it lacked a mathematical frame of reference. The fact of the matter is that there are many important fields of investigation to which mathematics is not applicable, or is applicable only to a very limited extent.

Furthermore, even where its application is both relevant and useful, measurement usually has an element of error in it. Even the most exact description or measurement a scientist can make is still only approximate. Even if a particular measurement were quite free of error and wholly exact, replications of the measurement would almost certainly fail to yield identical measures. We saw earlier in this regard that different observers will have different perceptions and conceptions and will view somewhat differently what we call the "same" situation.

Mathematical models can never incorporate all factors in the real world, nor can they ever supply precise answers to non-

---

[48] Oliver Benson, "The Use of Mathematics in the Study of Political Science," in Charlesworth, *Mathematics and the Social Sciences*, p. 56.

mathematical questions.[49] Models are never a substitute for theory. Either explanation or evaluation may be elucidated by models, but models themselves do not explain or evaluate. Explanation is a function of theory: models may have heuristic value in suggesting ways in which various elements interact but they do not explain the interactions.[50] When models are of no particular help, the failing most often responsible is likely to be oversimplification. We noted earlier that science always simplifies because reality can never be replicated in all of its complexity; however, it is a failing if the model simplifies in the wrong way or in the wrong places.[51] Other things being equal, simplicity is a virtue, but models can be misleading when important variables are omitted or neglected.

Another failing of models lies in undue stress on exactness and rigor at the expense of content and meaning. Models may be improperly exact, calling for measures that cannot in fact be obtained.[52] The usefulness of a model depends on a firm grasp of both its inherent properties and the empirical conditions to which the model is going to be applied. Above all, the temptation to force empirical data to fit the model must be consciously resisted throughout the inquiry.[53] Any model must be the servant, not the master, of interpretation. A model is a particular mode of representation; it always has some irrelevant features. Since models abstract from reality, we can make use of several models even when they are not compatible with one another. As Abraham Kaplan remarks, models may be beautiful but they may have their secret vices.[54] Presumably this is true of both social science models and their counterparts in the world of fashion.

The social scientist should avoid the extremism of excessive zeal or total repudiation in his attitude toward any method-

---

[49] Ibid., p. 32.

[50] Eugene Meehan, *Contemporary Political Thought: A Critical Study* (Homewood, Ill.: Dorsey Press, 1967). p. 294.

[51] Kaplan, *Conduct of Inquiry,* p. 281.

[52] Ibid., p. 283.

[53] Ibid., p. 291.

[54] Ibid., p. 288.

ological tool, mathematical or nonmathematical. He should avoid both the mystiques of quantity and quality in his attitude toward the study of social and political phenomena. The mystique of quantity is an exagggerated regard for the significance of measurement, simply because it is quantitative, without regard to what is being measured or to what can be done with the results of such measurement. Number is treated as having some intrinsic scientific value, almost as if numbers were the repositories of occult powers.[55]

There is a corresponding mystique of quality, illustrated by the previous discussion of Jacques Ellul, which maintains that counting and measuring cannot capture the qualitative characteristics of man and society. To such opponents of quantification, a kind of black magic seems to inhere in numbers. To them, counting seems pointless at best, and at worst, is a hopeless distortion of what is truly important in the study of man and society. As Ellul argues, some of the critics believe that the end result is the development of a mentality which employs such techniques for evil ends.

The difficulty with such discourse is the manner in which it polarizes the two modes of inquiry. The point is that both quality and quantity are misconceived when they are taken to be antithetical or even alternative. After all, quantities are of qualities of some kind (although measurement is always subject to some limitations, as we have seen). A quantitative property is a quality to which a number has been assigned ("quality" here meaning a descriptive property). Mathematical operations cannot increase the precision of initial measurements. Nevertheless, many social scientists seem to imagine that they enhance the exactitude of their statements merely by putting mathematical formulae on paper. One consequence of this fetishist worship of quantitative technique for the sake of technique is that the reviews of such political science research by professional mathematicians are often devastating.

C. Wright Mills once wrote about the kind of social scien-

---

[55] Ibid., p. 172.

tist who would love to wear a white coat with an IBM symbol of some sort on the breast pocket. Such scholars are out to do with society and history what they believe physicists have done with nature. Mills went on to say:

> This rational and empty optimism reveals a profound ignorance of the role of ideas in human history, the nature of power and its relations to knowledge, and of the meaning of moral action and the place of knowledge within it. Among the Scientists, the most frequent type is The Higher Statistician, who breaks down truth and falsity into such fine particles that we cannot tell the difference between them. By the costly rigor of their methods, they succeed in trivializing men and society, and in the process, their own minds as well. . . . Research technicians are going to have to go about their work with more imaginative concern for its larger meanings, as well as with mathematical ingenuity.[56]

There is no reason to think that Mills meant to sneer at the use of mathematical modes of social analysis. His intellectual thrust was directed against the notion that "science advances in the last decimal point." For although quantification has its merits, it is neither a necessary nor a sufficient condition for science. Many concepts are significant without being numbered. A discipline that formulates and tests laws and theories is a science, whether or not they are expressed in the form of equations. Mills was objecting to quantification at the price of significance; the refusal to describe, explain, and understand the wider areas of human behavior in society.[57] Mills stood squarely opposed to social science " as a set of bureaucratic techniques which inhibit social inquiry by 'methodological' pretensions, which congest such work by obscurantist conceptions, or which trivialize it by concern with minor problems unconnected with publicly relevant issues."[58]

One can readily great the truth of the statement by Herbert Butterfield that "without the achievements of the mathemati-

---

[56] C. Wright Mills, *Power, Politics and People*, edited by Irving Louis Horowitz (New York: Oxford University Press, 1963), pp. 569 and 576.

[57] Ibid., p. 570.

[58] C. Wright Mills, *The Sociological Imagination* (New York: Oxford University Press, 1959), p. 20.

cians, the scientific revolution, as we know it, would have been impossible."[59] Nevertheless, not every method is equally useful in studying every kind of problem. Even the most highly successful quantitative techniques and formal models will not, by themselves, provide solutions to the questions which political thinkers have raised since the time of Plato and Aristotle. Answers to such questions depend ultimately on a philosophical view of the world and of the human beings who live in it. The scientific method is designed for the study of what is, and it cannot be used to study what ought to be. It can yield data and reliable knowledge about how politics does work. To argue for any one philosophical view, one requires the maximum possible reference to the body of knowledge accumulated so painfully through the ages.

We are living in a period when hopes are high for more precision, more accurate measurement, and perhaps some degree of predictability in the various social science disciplines. Yet the portion of the subject matter of political science that lends itself to measurement covers only a part of the area with which political scientists may be justifiably concerned. Large scale political and social processes are still very much a focus of attention for students of comparative political systems and international relations. Karl W. Deutsch has wisely said: "All analytic work in the social sciences is primarily tied to judgments of relevance ... the advice to study more mathematics should be tempered with the insistence that they [the younger social scientists] will have to judge the relevance of their models against their fund of factual knowledge *as social scientists*. No amount of mathematical knowledge or advice can take this task from their shoulders."[60] Professor Deutsch offers this advice from a background which includes extensive work in mathematical analysis.

Mathematical techniques may be a useful tool in the

---

[59] Herbert Butterfield, *The Origins of Modern Science 1300-1800* (New York: Macmillan, 1950), p. 77.

[60] Karl W. Deutsch, *The Nerves of Government: Models of Political Communication and Control* (New York: Free Press, 1963), p. 43.

organization of data but they are never in themselves a means to their explanation. Both the partisans and the opponents of quantitative social science research sometimes seem to forget this rather obvious fact. Social science has had its share of trends and fads. It is quite possible that the exaggeration of quantification as a means of attaining "objectivity" will be looked upon as a temporary aberration in the next generation of social scientists. Even if it is fully agreed that, properly used, mathematics can be of signal aid to inquiry, one is entitled to considerable skepticism about many of the attempted applications of mathematics in the social sciences today.[61]

In addition to mere decoration, there are other ways of employing mathematics spuriously. One of them can be seen in work where the premises and conclusions are stated verbally and amount to exactly the same thing couched in different ways. Elaborate calculations may be inserted in between the verbalism but are quite superfluous to the whole argument. Loose and muddled thinking can thus be concealed in a cloak of pretended exactitude. Dubious assumptions stated in conventional language do not become more adequate merely because they are translated into mathematical language. The very precision and formal elegance possible in mathematics can blind some analysts to what they are actually doing.

The moral of all this is that we should not take the mathematical formulae in social science at their face value, but inquire whether they in fact serve some purpose other than the desire to dazzle the reader. It is worth noting that writers on social phenomena who are mathematicians do not obtrude mathematics needlessly into their work. For example, the writings of Bertrand Russell bear no traces of this failing. To refuse to deal with important and interesting problems simply because the relevant factors cannot be measured would condemn social science to sterility.

There is nothing wrong in attempting to make our knowl-

---

[61] Kurt W. Back, "The Game and the Myth as Two Languages of Social Science," *Behavioral Science,* vol. 8 (1963), p. 70.

edge of society as rigorous as possible, providing such formulations do actually enhance our comprehension of human behavior. Any efforts to enlarge the scope of application of political science are worth making. The differences between the natural and the social sciences are not accidental and are not readily removed simply by the application of "naturalistic" methodologies to social phenomena. The subject matter of the social sciences is inherently more complicated in the sense that we have more variables to deal with than in physics or biology.

Morris R. Cohen has summarized the greater complexity of social facts as connected with (1) their less repeatable character, (2) their less direct observability, (3) their greater variability and lesser uniformity, and (4) the greater difficulty of isolating one factor at a time.[62] The units of the social sciences do not permit simple addition because the central questions involve answers relating to both men and institutions. The difficulties are compounded in political science because we are committed to the study of vast aggregates of men, that is, political institutions.

In a more recent essay, Gunnar Myrdal follows in the footsteps of Cohen when he says:

> . . . the study of social facts and relationships really must concern much more complex and fluid matters than facts and relationships in nature. In social study we do not have the constants similar to those of the natural sciences which is an indication of the deeper truth that, in our field, human institutions and attitudes are prominent in the causal relationships. These phenomena can be represented only very partially by parameters and variables in simplified models of causal relationships; indeed, they are much more difficult even to observe and measure as facts. . . . In emulating the methods of the natural sciences, we exclude from consideration everything related to the fact that human beings have souls. Specifically, we tend not to appreciate the fact that people live in a complex system of institutions which manifest sharply

---

[62] Morris R. Cohen, *Reason and Nature* (Glencoe, Ill.: Free Press, 1953), p. 351. For the entire discussion of the differences between the natural and social sciences, see pp. 333-68.

differentiated combinations of changeability and rigidity, according
to the attitudes that have been molded by . . . these institutions.[63]

Regardless of the method adopted to pursue inquiry,
values of the investigator play a crucial role in selecting, guiding, and interpreting the research which flows out of the
methodology. Research is an idea without form or content
until particular values are stated. Methodological ingenuity and
technical finesse will not absolve us from having to make subjective judgments about the validity and meaning of the results
of our inquiry.

Heinz Eulau has argued that the notion of value-neutrality,
understood as the cultivation of a judicious attitude toward
values, has not been given a fair chance. There are inevitable
tensions in the two-way passage from science to values and
from values to science. Eulau comments:

The behavioral scientist . . . serves two masters: social values and
scientific values. His science demands of him a maximum of
truth and objectivity as means to scientific knowledge. Social purpose demands of him that he see to it that the consumers of his
knowledge use it with a maximum of realism and rationality. . . .
These two masters are not at loggerheads, they need not make
mutually contradictory demands on the scientist. For the scientist's
commitment to social purposes can best be implemented if he
serves well the demands of science, and he can best serve the
demands of science if he demonstrates judiciousness in regard to the
multiple uses to which his scientific knowledge may be put.[64]

There appears to be a growing disenchantment with the
moral neutrality school of social science, a belief that it has led
to a decline in vision and has been used as a hedge against responsibility. There is clearly a growing commitment not only
to applying what we know, but to understanding the social
processes which underlie this application. Detachment does

[63] Gunnar Myrdal, "The Social Sciences and Their Impact on Society,"
in Herman D. Stein, editor, *Social Theory and Social Invention* (Cleveland:
Press of Case Western University, 1968), pp. 148-49.

[64] Heinz Eulau, "Values in Behavioral Science: Neutrality Revisited,"
Antioch Review, vol. 28 (Summer 1968), p. 167.

not imply neutrality to contending forces in the environment of
social science research. As Dante Germino writes:

> Objectivity in political theory comes not from the vain attempt to
> avoid evaluation and thereby appear impartial but through the
> adoption of critical standards and criteria of evaluation that are not
> transitory and parochial but are based on an experientially sound
> anthropology. The theorist's objectivity is reflected in the quality
> and validity of his critical standards.[65]

The most fruitful research generally begins with an awareness
of some problem that is felt to be significant. It is curious that
in some quarters, in order to be regarded as a social scientist,
one must get as far away from the actual problems and operations of society as possible; yet by their work, all students of
man and society assume and imply moral and political decisions; work in social science has always been accompanied by
problems of evaluation.

So far as the problems are concerned, again the aim ought
to be clarity about the values according to which they are
selected and avoidance, as best one can, of any evaluative bias
in their solution. Of course, the social scientist should follow
wherever his solutions lead him, regardless of the moral or
political implications involved in his research. Anyone who
spends his life studying man and society and publishing the results is acting morally for good or ill and usually is acting politically as well. The question is whether he faces this condition
or whether he conceals it from himself and from others and
drifts morally. Some social scientists are afloat on a sea of
verbiage, claiming to be morally indifferent to the floating bits
of meaningless data which surround them.

Kenneth Boulding has said: "For all the attempts of our
positivists to dehumanize the sciences of man, a moral science
it remains."[66] The study of man contains a greater variety of

---

[65] Dante Germino, *Beyond Ideology: The Revival of Political Theory*
(New York: Harper and Row, 1967), p. 13.

[66] Kenneth Boulding, "Is Economics Necessary?" *Scientific Monthly*,
vol. 68 (April 1949), p. 240.

intellectual styles than any other area of cultural endeavor. How different scholars go about their work, and what they seek to accomplish by it, often do not seem to have any real common denominator. There are many ways of thinking, many conceptions and methods, ideas and notions that rub elbows together with varying degrees of discomfort. A wide variety of problems confront us, and each man addresses himself to the problems that he finds intrinsically interesting. Political science contains many men and women, many schools, many traditions, many methods, many issues. There is a kind of friendly competition among the diverse methods and approaches. There is a good chance that major contributions are going to be made by individual nonconformists rather than by the people who slavishly follow the currently fashionable methodological fads and approaches.

The foregoing account may, at times, have seemed confusing rather than enlightening to the reader. If this is true to an extent, it is no doubt due in part to "the tyranny of words" that we discussed earlier in the section on the language of political science. Much of the confusion and contradiction is in the situation itself. There is no use attempting to conceal the fact that there are serious differences of outlook among political scientists. There are contradictions and tensions within the discipline which will continue to evolve as we move toward the end of the century.[67]

The distinction between facts and values in the social sciences is extremely tenuous. Every fact in the social sciences which has any relevance is permeated with value; otherwise, why would we have chosen it for study? Social data are so infinitely numerous and diverse that any scientific study must select its facts in accordance with the needs of the problem and the method. If there is selection of data, there obviously must be a purpose in the selection, whether conscious or unconscious.

---

[67] For a fascinating glimpse of some social scientists at work anticipating this event, see *"Toward the Year 2000: Work in Progress," Daedalus,* vol. 96 (Summer 1967).

Ordinarily, one would expect that the criteria for selecting a research subject have something to do with the contemporary social importance of the subject matter. Hans J. Morgenthau has pointed out that current intellectual concerns regarding the plight of the poor owe their origin to a radical change in our intellectual perspectives on the causes and cures of poverty in society.[68] Judgments as to what is or is not important are involved in the formulation of all research. To detect practical problems is to make evaluations.

Analysis begins with moral content; in political life that which is significant can only be understood in moral terms. David Apter summarizes this viewpoint in the following trenchant passage:

> There is a difference between scientific work in the social sciences and in the natural sciences . . . a difference in moral point of view, as related to persons, their obligations, and their desires. This constitutes the uniqueness of social science. Even if we could account for all the variables in social conduct, we would still have to deal with the *meaning* of social acts. The consequences of that meaning and the inferences to be drawn from it form the basis of political analysis. Does this mean that beyond science lies moral intuition, that Humpty Dumpty of human experience? I believe the answer is yes. Knowledge of experience requires the total commitment of all our senses.[69]

Apter's statement underscores the fact that the social scientist is not suddenly confronted with the need to choose values; he is already working on the basis of certain values. The first of these is simply the value of truth. All social scientists, by the fact of their existence, are involved in the struggle between enlightenment and ignorance. Of course, the truth of our findings may or may not be relevant to human affairs. There are degrees of relevance in this regard.

---

[68] Quoted in James C. Charlesworth, editor, *A Design for Political Science: Scope, Objectives, and Methods* (Philadelphia: American Academy of Political and Social Science, 1966), p. 142.

[69] David Apter, *The Politics of Modernization* (Chicago: University of Chicago Press, 1965), p. xiv.

Apter's stress on meaning as the basis of political analysis should be carefully pondered by the student of comparative politics. All interpretation of meaning strives for clarity and verifiable accuracy of insight and comprehension. In a short story, one character asks the other: "What does it all mean: Life, everything?" The person replies: "It doesn't *mean* anything; it just is." This feeling of meaninglessness and emptiness has been labeled as the "existential vacuum" by the psychiatrist, Dr. Viktor E. Frankl. There are people who cannot see any meaning and purpose in their lives. This sense of anomie, which afflicts many in our generation, has the most profound political and sociological implications.

Dr. Frankl presents a thesis that is quite relevant to this discussion of value preferences and commitments. He maintains that each situation implies a unique meaning. Man's search for meaning is a primary force in his life and not a "secondary rationalization" of instinctual drives. There are purposes to achieve and meanings to fulfill. Yet, as Alfred North Whitehead remarked: "Many a scientist has patiently designed experiments for the *purpose* of substantiating his belief that animal operations are motivated by no purpose."[70]

Dr. Frankl points out that the problem of meaning and purpose cannot be omitted from the study of human behavior. He writes:

> Man has a capacity for self-transcendence. It is not true that man is concerned only with satisfying drives, gratifying instincts, restoring his inner equilibrium. This is a caricature of man. Being human always means pointing to, being directed toward something other than yourself. . . . The gas chambers of Auschwitz were a consequence of the theory that man is nothing but the product of heredity and environment. They were ultimately prepared not in some ministry in Berlin but rather at the desks and in the lecture halls of nihilistic scientists and philosophers.[71]

---

[70] Alfred North Whitehead, *The Function of Reason* (Princeton: Princeton University Press, 1929), p. 12.

[71] Viktor E. Frankl, *Man's Search for Meaning: An Introduction to Logotherapy* (New York: Washington Square Press, 1967), pp. 164-65.

Dr. Frankl is no armchair thinker; his observations are forti-
fied by his record of three years spent in Auschwitz and Dachau
where he lost his first wife and his entire family, except for a
sister. In an incredible demonstration of the human spirit, he
emerged from this experience wholly unembittered and developed his unique theory of logotherapy.

Arnold Toynbee has said that some civilizations have
killed themselves by virtue of the values they chose. This must
surely be a sobering observation for social scientists to con-
template as they carry on their scholarship and public policy
activities. There are some areas of life (and none more so than
the areas of our ultimate values) in which one simply cannot
afford to make mistakes. The nihilistic notion that "anything
goes" in the area of values simply because one happens to think
it is right is a kind of grand error still too frequently heard in
social sciences discourse. Values are not arbitrary nor are they
merely a matter of what a person or a people happens to desire.
Values are objective at least in the sense that they are objects
of rational discourse. Values are not either absolute or relative; they are always *both* absolute and relative. Huston Smith
has developed this idea in a persuasive way. He writes:

> Values are always relative to someone or some group, but for that
> person or group they are absolute. . . . To say that values are
> relative doesn't make them viciously so; it doesn't make them sub-
> jective or dependent on taste or whim. . . . There are values which
> apply to human beings across the cultures and which are absolute
> for them because they relate to the generic human situation.[72]

Professor Smith points out that one of the "cross-cultural
values" noted above pertains to the human infant. In every
culture we know, it is indispensable for the health and matura-
tion of a human being that he be surrounded by an atmosphere
of love and affection in his childhood years. Infants isolated
from love and attention grow up to be less than human; they

---

[72] See Huston Smith, "On Ethical Relativism," in Charles F. Madden,
editor, *Talks with Social Scientists* (Carbondale, Ill.: Southern Illinois University Press, 1968), pp. 120 and 123.

grow into subhuman animals, lacking personality and the capacity for responsive action. Psychologist William Sheldon has said: "More fundamental in man than the drive for prestige or wealth or power or sexual gratification is the need embedded in the human makeup for the sense of right-orientation."[73]

The problem of the relativity of values is very complex, and cannot be treated adequately in any summary way. When the anthropologists finished tallying up the variations in customs and beliefs over the face of the globe, we had striking evidence for the great plasticity of human behavior. Values seemed hopelessly relative to the society in which they were practiced. Some anthropologists were never comfortable with the idea of complete relativity, for it seemed to destroy the possibilities of finding scientific regularities upon which to base some kind of moral action. For example, Clyde Kluckhohn thought that values were not wholly relativistic, but rested on uniformities responsible for the human condition.[74]

Cultural relativism emphasizes the differences among cultures and asserts there is little possibility of moral communication among them. Today this appears to be a retrogressive doctrine. Scholars are seeking to bridge cultural barriers rather than emphasize the difference among cultures in their research. They are discovering that men do share many values across cultures. Contextually, values lose their absolute relativity. As we apply scientific method to all realms of human activities, we will be able to establish broader interrelationships among social phenomena and diminish further the area of relativity of values. As we come to understand how and why certain types of social structures affect man, it is not unreasonable to expect that morality will tend to standardize and universalize.

"Universality" of values need not mean authoritarianism of values. As Ernest Becker says: "The extreme relativists championed their position precisely because it seemed to guar-

---

[73] Quoted by Smith, Ibid., p. 125.
[74] Clyde Kluckhohn, *Culture and Behavior,* edited by Richard Kluckhohn (New York: Free Press, 1962).

antee a freedom from the right set of values. Today . . . pluralistic society is uncomfortably monolithic in its irrationality; it is plural without a guiding plan. But what if uniform institutional arrangements that respond to intellectual control are the only way of guaranteeing a multiplicity of personal values?"[75] Rather than leading to chaos, a standardized morality based on universal values could be a major source of dependable order.

Today, however, society has a multiplicity of conflicting moral values. Societies are multivalent and members who mature within them are also multivalent. The complexities of this situation lead some observers to speak of society as a jungle.[76] In coping with the problems which emerge in a diversified society, we shall require judgment, common sense, independent knowledge, and the elusive quality of political wisdom. Although in one sense every age is an age of crisis, there are periods in the lives of those communities we call nations subject to stress when they are confronted with unusually critical problems. We live in such an era, when institutions are seriously challenged and attempts are made to change radically the traditional images of man and his society and culture.[77]

Unless we are willing to turn the whole matter over to the unknown forces of biological evolution, social scientists simply must concern themselves with values. For in our time, such values as reason and freedom are in obvious peril. We are, perhaps, at the ending of an epoch: our basic definitions of society and self are being overtaken by new realities. Many of our major orientations have virtually collapsed as adequate explanations of the world and ourselves.

To formulate any problem requires that we state the values involved and the threat to those values. The future of human

---

[75] Ernest Becker, *The Structure of Evil: An Essay on the Justification of the Science of Man* (New York: George Braziller, 1968), p. 395.

[76] Alfred McClung Lee, *Multivalent Man* (New York: George Braziller, 1966), p. vii.

[77] William Barrett, *Irrational Man: A Study in Existential Philosophy* (New York: Doubleday, 1958).

affairs is not merely some set of variables to be predicted. On the contrary, the future is what is to be decided, within the limits of historical possibility, of course. One of the tasks confronting the social scientist is to formulate choices and subject them to critical analysis.

Social scientists can thus clarify the meaning and the consequences of values and attempt to ascertain and order priorities among competing values. Some values cannot exist in simple juxtaposition, and we are forced to choose between them. The social scientist can illuminate the relevant data involved in this decision-making process by using the tools and insights of his discipline. F. S. C. Northrop has asserted that both legal and ethical experience are much more complex than the traditional theory of these subjects would lead one to suppose.[78] Social scientists should not abdicate their responsibility to grapple with this complexity in their scholarship and public policy activities. "Objectivity" should not be construed as granting exemption from social responsibility.

Some social scientists have expressed awareness of the possible harmful social implications of social-science knowledge.[79] Knowledge is power, and that power confronts us with dangers and presents us with opportunities. Knowledge is not virtue: it is the power to do good and evil alike. There is no guarantee whatever that the true and the good always go hand in hand. Social science can advance us to the point where we can intelligently order our values in accord with our basic convictions regarding what is good in life.

To conclude this section on values and modes of thought, the following quotation from James Bryant Conant, former President of Harvard University, seems fitting. Dr. Conant maintains that just as a man needs two legs to walk on, the social sciences need two types of thinkers. He writes:

---

[78] F. S. C. Northrop, *The Complexity of Legal and Ethical Experience* (Boston: Little, Brown, 1959).

[79] Arnold M. Rose, *Theory and Method in the Social Sciences* (Minneapolis: University of Minnesota Press, 1954), p. 187.

A free society requires today among its teachers, professors, and practitioners two types of individuals: the one prefers the empirical-inductive method of inquiry; the other the theoretical-deductive outlook. Both modes of thought have their dangers; both have their advantages. In any given profession, in any single institution, in any particular country, the one mode may be underdeveloped or overdeveloped; if so, the balance will need redressing. Above all, the continuation of intellectual freedom requires a tolerance of the activities of the proponents of the one mode by the other . . . to meet the needs of a free and highly industrialized society.[80]

---

[80] James Bryant Conant, *Two Modes of Thought* (New York: Trident Press, 1964), pp. xxxi and 95.

SIX

New Horizons for Comparative Politics

The systematic study of comparative government began with an historical and theoretical examination of the legal institutions of the democracies of Western Europe and North America. This rather narrow focus concealed from view a large number of variables and permitted the elaboration of a body of integrated theoretical insights. However, focusing analysis on the formal institutions of government slighted the nonpolitical determinants of political behavior and the nonpolitical bases of governmental institutions. Very little attention was given to the informal arrangements of society and their role in the exercise of political power and decision-making.

More specifically, the traditional approach to Western political systems focused on the formal constitutional aspects such as chief executives, parliaments, civil services, and electoral systems. This emphasis upon formal legal arrangements was an outgrowth of the positivistic reaction to historicism. The historicist approach was mainly a matter of abstract and formal speculation upon the broadest conceivable questions, with little regard for the empirical content of the speculation. The positivist reaction to this approach stressed hard facts in the form of legal and institutional empirical data. The concern with factual description gave the discipline a concrete framework and a substantive foundation from which to jump off into new areas of scholarly inquiry and more intensive analysis of the empirical data that were so painfully collected.

Perhaps the great strength of comparative politics during this period of formal comparison within accepted traditional categories was the relative homogeneity of the nations being studied. North America and Western Europe share a complex of values, outlooks, and technology. This emphasis on the homogeneous elements did ignore a large number of economic, cultural, and historical variables which would later be dissected by scholars as they began to explore new areas of inquiry. Departing from the legal framework and method, scholars began to probe into the nonlegal levels and processes of politics. A substantial literature developed from this perspective concerning such relatively unexplored areas as pressure groups, public opinion, and political behavior. The machinery of functioning political systems was subjected to intensive analysis. Scholars turned away from a purely formal and constitutional approach to a consideration of political dynamics and the processes of decision-making.[1]

As a result of the expanded scope of comparative analysis, there has been a torrential outpouring of literature on comparative politics since the end of the Second World War. The field of comparative politics has been greatly affected by the extension of inquiry into Asia, Africa, Southeast Asia, Latin America, and the Middle East. Some of the traditional questions and problems now seem almost irrelevant as a result of the expanded scope of inquiry. Among other things, inquiry into the changing politics of the non-Western world pointed up the inadequacy of traditional approaches which did not take into account critically important social and cultural factors.[2]

---

[1] William A. Welsh, *Studying Politics* (New York: Praeger, 1973), pp. 39-40.

[2] See James F. Downs, *Cultures in Crisis* (Beverly Hills, Calif.: Glencoe Press, 1971), pp. 29-30.

In studying non-Western political systems we began to deal not only with strange societies but also with ideas and values often incompatible with those of the West. To compare externals without a profound understanding of their sociocultural context is to invite the accumulation of highly misleading political data. Accumulation of unrelated information on individual political systems can hardly be considered the hallmark of comparative analysis. Political study which ignores the total fabric of society is likely to be unproductive.[3]

To find categories and concepts appropriate for the comparison of political systems differing radically in culture and structure has become a central quest for comparative politics as a discipline. *Comparative Politics,* a journal founded in 1968 for the purpose of publishing articles devoted to comparative analysis, listed some of the newer concepts: role structure, political culture, political system, consensus, actors, socialization, rationality, structural-functional analysis, and ideal types.[4] The search for new concepts reflects a drift toward the behavioral approach. As for analytic categories, we can see the ready availability of a stock of paradigms, developed to give students of comparative politics convenient sets of tools for analysis. Political scientists continue elaborate new analytic categories designed to expand the range of political inquiry to include many components of the social process.

One of the more difficult issues involved in methodological reevaluation is determining the boundaries between the political system and the total social order of which it is a part. The kinds of structures that control the boundaries of the political system are of the utmost importance in the functioning of each system. The boundaries between the society and the political system differ from one political system to another. People may find it necessary to accept new forms for the polity; to achieve these conditions it may be necessary to alter the social structure while

[3] See Lawrence C. Mayer, *Comparative Political Inquiry: A Methodological Survey* (Homewood, Ill.: Dorsey Press, 1972), p. 163.

[4] *Comparative Politics,* vol. 1, no. 1 (October 1968), p. 1.

developing new political attitudes. New institutions may have to be created and consolidated.[5]

Whatever the scope of their work, contemporary students of comparative politics are the new general theorists of political science. They are seeking generalizations about all political systems, regardless of national and cultural boundaries. They are searching for general patterns of politics which transcend time and place, for elements common to all political systems as opposed to those which vary with culture and experience.[6] An extraordinary enrichment of the discipline of political science has resulted from the inclusion of non-Western political systems. Their inclusion in comparative analysis is to political science what a new, more powerful telescope is to astronomy: it expands the range and scope of the inquiry.

There appears to be a consensus among students of comparative politics that a comparative political science must be crosscultural as well as crossnational. The logic underlying this viewpoint is clear: Crossnational studies tend to be culture bound. The optimists in comparative politics believe that a large number of generalizations (true for all cultures) will be discovered and will be relevant to practical problems in each particular culture. The felt need is to develop a crosscultural science to test theories against the behavior of people in other cultures. Needless to say, the profound differences among non-Western countries and between them and the West pose sharply the problem of comparability.[7]

Almond and Coleman have questioned the foregoing proposition by claiming that the differences between Western and non-Western systems have been exaggerated in many ways. They argue that all the types of political structures which

---

[5] See Alex Inkeles and David H. Smith, *Becoming Modern: Individual Change in Six Developing Countries* (Cambridge, Mass.: Harvard University Press, 1974).

[6] Alan C. Isaak, *Scope and Methods of Political Science* (Homewood, Ill.: Dorsey Press, 1975), especially Chapter 6, "Generalizations in Political Science," pp. 83-104.

[7] See Dankwart A. Rustow, "Modernization and Comparative Politics," in *Comparative Politics*, vol. 1, no. 1 (October 1968), pp. 37-51.

are to be found in modern systems are also found in the non-Western and the more primitive ones (although the latter may be characterized by intermittent interactions rather than regularized ones). They isolate four characteristics which they claim are located in all political systems and in terms of which these systems may be compared. These "common properties of political systems" are specified as:

1. All political systems, including the most simple, have political structure. They may be compared to one another according to the degree and form of structural specialization.

2. The same functions are performed in all political systems, even though these functions may be performed with different frequencies and by different kinds of structures. Comparisons may be made according to the frequency of the performance of the functions, the kinds of structures performing them, and the style of their performance.

3. All political structure, no matter how specialized, is multifunctional, whether it is found in primitive or in modern societies.

4. All political systems are "mixed" systems in the cultural sense. There are no "all-modern" cultures and structures, in the sense of rationality, and no "all-primitive" ones in the sense of traditionality. They differ in the relative dominance of the one as against the other, and in the pattern of mixture of the two components.[8]

Using this classification scheme, they argue that all of the functions performed by the American political system are also performed by an East African tribe. There is no such thing as a society that maintains internal and external order which has no political structure (legitimate patterns of interaction by means of which the order is maintained).

A fundamental objective of comparative political analysis today is the elaboration of refined, generalized phenomena of the political process common to all systems. To reach for this objective we must first hypothesize a set of universals of political behavior, followed by the empirical validation of this alleged

---

[8] Gabriel Almond and James S. Coleman, *The Politics of the Developing Areas* (Princeton: Princeton University Press, 1960), p. 11. To see how Almond modified this original scheme in the light of criticism, see Gabriel Almond and G. Bingham Powell, Jr., *Comparative Politics: A Developmental Approach* (Boston: Little, Brown, 1966).

universality. As Almond and Coleman put the point: ". . . in our efforts to establish the properties of political systems, compare them with each other, and classify them into types, we explicitly separate structure from function, structure from culture, social systems from political systems, empirical properties from their normative implications."[9] The comparative method can be employed more rigorously not only in cross-national comparisons, but in subnational and international system comparisons as well.

Increasingly, therefore, political scientists are asking questions about the characteristics of the political system and its performance. They are investigating how particular laws and institutions function in the context of a particular political and social system (or how it could be expected to function if transferred into the context of some other system.[10])

Largely because of the widening scope of the field, units for analysis have changed with almost bewildering rapidity. The units of analysis employed in the past have consisted mainly of parties, government, parliaments, armies, and bureaucracies with their various specialized subgroups. These units of analysis were invariably considered in the context of Western nation-states. In recent years, the units of analysis have been expanded greatly in order to encompass the phenomena of non-Western systems. Kinship, family structures, tribes, and language groups suddenly become relevant. Behavioral analysis focuses on microunits; that is, the individual and the small group. The key unit for analysis is the interacting individual as shaped by social influences. Political processes stem essentially from the large number of interpersonal relations that relate to the exercise of power and influence. Such analysis permits the treatment of a number of variables that are sometimes neglected by other political scientists.[11]

---

[9] Almond and Coleman, *The Politics of the Developing Areas,* p. 13.

[10] Mayer, *Comparative Political Inquiry,* pp. 86-87.

[11] See Arthur S. Banks and Robert B. Textor, *A Cross-Polity Survey* (Cambridge, Mass.: M.I.T. Press, 1963). In this study, a computer was used to compare all of the 115 independent governments in the world.

The new theoretical approaches to political phenomena permitted scholars to dissolve such an entity as a nation into a much larger array of components and subsystems within it. At the same time, a much larger number of significant variables or relevant conditions came into play. New data have become available on a rapidly increasing scale. There are millions of computer cards containing political data of various types. It has been estimated that there are five million such cards added every year. It is clear that the process of ordering and associating these data depends on computer technology for storage and retrieval.

The very diversity of the new data is creating a major research problem. Work is under way to prepare profiles of the distribution of many of these variables within particular political systems. This will make it possible to compare the international and intranational distribution patterns of important variables. It is possible to study such patterns of variables not only among states or territories but also among organizations, social groups, and classes. We are now concerned with sampling the total universe of man's experiments with politics, contemporary and historical; national, subnational, and international. We concentrate on environmental influences on politics, political influences on the environment, and the interaction of political variables with each other. [12]

The most notable trend in political science in recent years has been the attempt to place the study of political institutions in a broader context of social structure, cultural orientation, and psychological dynamics. This trend will likely continue with greater refinement and sophistication in future years. It might be noted in passing that the changes which have occurred could not have materialized without a large increase in the pool of available data, available research techniques, and of skilled personnel in political science. As noted above, the proliferation

---

[12] Robert T. Holt and John E. Turner, *The Methodology of Comparative Research* (New York: Free Press 1970). This book contains a wealth of insight into the problems confronting comparative research. It is particularly stimulating in its treatment of cross-cultural research and competing paradigms in comparative politics.

of data has created an information crisis. If this material is not to overwhelm us, it must be organized around conceptual systems capable of making significant theoretical generalizations. Without such organization, crude empiricism threatens to run rampant.[13]

There are scholars who argue that we have reached the point where further conceptualization may become counterproductive. Others maintain that the behavioral revolution was so successful that we are neglecting the institutional configurations that were so important in traditional comparative politics.[14] One of the problems which will confront us is the relationship of configurative analysis to comparability. By *configurative analysis* is meant the identification and interpretation of factors in the whole social order which appear to affect the workings of the political system. This mode of analysis may also be referred to as *contextual* or *cultural* analysis.[15] The universe of data employed in configurative analysis is as limitless as the universe of knowledge. For each political system there are variables running into the thousands. Ralph Braibanti has argued that the least developed aspect of comparative analysis is the identification and evaluation of configurative factors in terms of function and institution. He further suggests that it is the most important aspect, raising difficult methodological problems that might well receive a share of our attention.[16]

If comparative political methodology is to accommodate the elements of configurative analysis, political science must create ways to integrate configurative data in that methodology. As a result of this union, comparative politics could become the

[13] See the introductory chapter in Roy C. Macridis and Bernard Brown, *Comparative Politics: Notes and Readings*, fifth edition (Homewood, Ill.: Dorsey Press, 1977), pp. 10-11.

[14] See Guy Peters, John C. Doughtie, and M. Kathleen McCulloch, "Types of Democratic Systems and Types of Public Policy: An Empirical Examination," *Comparative Politics*, vol. 9, no. 3 (April 1977), p. 327.

[15] See James A. Bill and Robert L. Hardgrave, Jr., *Comparative Politics: The Quest for Theory* (Columbus, Ohio: Merrill, 1973), p. 12.

[16] Ralph Braibanti, "Comparative Political Analytics Reconsidered," *Journal of Politics*, vol. 30 (February 1968), p. 53.

paramount interpreter of political behavior within the milieu of culture. The classic relationship between comparative politics and political theory may be reestablished. Carried through to their logical conclusions, the trends discussed in this section point in the direction of a unified theory of politics.

Comparative analysis yields rich knowledge and insights about significant regularities and differences in the working of political systems and in political behavior. Equally important, comparative research broadens our conceptions of the multiple ways in which similar outcomes of political behavior result from highly diverse structures and culturally varied forms of activity. When quantitative and qualitative growth occur at such extraordinary rates in a discipline, our theoretical frameworks and conceptual vocabularies are often strained beyond their capacity to codify and assimilate the new findings and insights of research.[17] It has been pointed out that among the several fields into which political science is usually divided, comparative politics is the only one that carries a methodological label. Comparative politics indicates the how but not the what of the analysis.[18] In the years ahead, analytical sophistication, empirical techniques, and descriptive knowledge will need to be effectively integrated in a theoretical context. The comparative approach is as old as political science, but there is now a pressing need to integrate, synthesize, and reconceptualize the vast literature on political systems that has been generated by scholars working on the frontiers of the discipline.

---

[17] See the witty but serious essay by Jorgen Rasmussen, "Once You've Made a Revolution, Everything's the Same," in George J. Graham, Jr., and George W. Carey, editors, *The Post-Behavioral Era: Perspectives on Political Science* (New York: David McKay, 1972), pp. 71-87. Rasmussen suggests that we have reached the point where further conceptualization becomes counterproductive.

[18] Arend Lijphart, "Comparative Politics and the Comparative Method," in Macridis and Brown, *Comparative Politics, Notes and Readings*, pp. 50-66.

SEVEN

The Evaluation of Political Systems

Eugene Meehan writes: "The inadequacy of political evaluation underlines one of the more glaring weaknesses in political science—its failure to deal adequately with the consequences of politics for society as a whole and for individual members of society."[1] We need to know far more than we do about the effect of politics on the various dimensions of human life. In the last analysis, the most important thing about any political system is its consequences for the members of society. As these words are written, public reports are issued by various sources revealing the corruption of public officials, judges, and the police. Apparently, even those who make the laws, and those in charge of enforcing them, do not feel bound by their authority. Governments themselves are investigating their own criminal activities. This is hardly the time to be locked in the stocks of a purported ethical neutrality. Both the advanced industrial nations and the emerging nations are coping with serious problems that portend real alterations in social and political policies directly affecting the lives of their citizenry.[2]

---

[1] Eugene Meehan, *Contemporary Political Thought* (Homewood, Ill.: Dorsey Press, 1967), p. 352.

[2] W. W. Rostow, *Politics and the Stages of Growth* (Cambridge: Cambridge University Press, 1971), p. 1.

Granting the necessity of political and social evaluation, it is not easy to evaluate the performance of political systems. What is a healthy political system? For what symptoms does the political pathologist look when he suspects that a system is unhealthy? What are the causes of the various syndromes to which a system may be vulnerable? What do we mean when we describe a political system as sound or unsound? All of these questions are problematic: the most dangerous political ailments are often the most difficult to diagnose.

There is bound to be disagreement as to precisely what society expects political activities to accomplish. Society must fulfill many functions and accommodate many competing claims. Political structures owe their stability and continuity to the support they receive from systems of belief, values, and symbolism. Such patterns of cultural support create a sense of legitimacy among the citizens. If a system maintains itself, it is likely to be relatively legitimate and generally accepted. There will be congruence between the goals of the system and the goals which the members of the polity prefer. Lack of acceptance means lack of consensus on fundamental goals; the resulting tensions may tear at the fabric of the political order.

According to Robert Dahl, three elements are required to judge how well a given political system performs. These are:

1. Criteria of value, worth, goodness, excellence, desirability;
2. Data about the behavior of the political system; and
3. Ways of applying the criteria to the behavior of the system in order to measure the degree of value, worth, goodness, excellence, and desirability attained.[3]

Few political scientists today address themselves to Aristotle's questions about the good man, the good citizen, the good polis, and the relations among them; yet, political study is very much concerned with the nature of man, the nature of the state, and the requirements of political obligation. Underlying every

---

[3] Robert A. Dahl, "The Evaluation of Political Systems," in Ithiel de Sola Pool, editor, *Contemporary Political Science* (New York: McGraw-Hill, 1967), p. 170.

Selected
Bibliography

1. The Scope of Comparative Political Analysis

Almond, Gabriel. *Political Development.* Boston: Little, Brown. 1970.
Almond, Gabriel and James Coleman, eds. *The Politics of the Developing Areas.* Princeton: Princeton University Press, 1960.
Braibanti, Ralph. "Comparative Political Analytics Reconsidered." *Journal of Politics,* vol. 30, February 1968, pp. 25-65.
Easton, David. *A Systems Analysis of Political Life.* New York: Wiley, 1965.
Edelman, Murray. *The Symbolic Uses of Politics.* Urbana: University of Illinois Press, 1964.
Merritt, Richard L. *Systematic Approaches to Comparative Politics.* Chicago: Rand McNally, 1970.
Roelofs, H. Mark. *The Language of Modern Politics: An Introduction to the Study of Government.* Homewood, Ill.: Dorsey Press, 1967.

2. Approaches to the Study of Comparative Politics

Cohen, Morris R. and Ernest Nagel. *An Introduction to Logic and Scientific Method.* New York: Harcourt, Brace, 1934.
Dahl, Robert A. "The Concept of Power." *Behavioral Science,* July 1957, pp. 201–15.
Easton, David, *The Political System.* New York: Knopf, 1953.
Eulau, Heinz. *The Behavioral Persuasion in Politics.* New York: Random House, 1965.

Fagen, Richard R. *Politics and Communication*. Boston: Little, Brown, 1966.

Finer, Herman. *The Theory and Practice of Modern Government*. New York: Holt, Rinehart and Winston, 1949.

Friedrich, Carl J. *Constitutional Government and Democracy*. Boston: Ginn, 1941.

Furniss, Edgar, Jr. *The Office of Premier in French Foreign Policy-Making*. Princeton, N. J.: Foreign Policy Analysis Project, 1954.

Gerth, Hans and C. Wright Mills. *Character and Social Structure*. New York: Harcourt, Brace and World, 1953.

Hyneman, Charles S. *The Study of Politics*. Urbana: University of Illinois Press, 1959.

Lasswell, Harold D. and Abraham Kaplan. *Power and Society: A Framework for Political Inquiry*. New Haven, Conn.: Yale University Press, 1950.

Macridis, Roy C. *The Study of Comparative Government*. New York: Doubleday, 1955.

March, James G. "The Power of Power." In David Easton, ed., *Varieties of Political Theory*. Englewood Cliffs, N. J.: Prentice-Hall, 1966.

MacIver, Robert M. *The Web of Government*. New York: Macmillan, 1951.

MacIver, Robert M. *Power Transformed*. New York: Macmillan, 1964.

Moore, Barrington, Jr. *Political Power and Social Theory*. Cambridge, Mass.: Harvard University Press, 1958.

Moore, Barrington, Jr. *The Social Origins of Dictatorship and Democracy*. Boston: Beacon Press, 1966.

Morgenthau, Hans J. "The Evils of Politics and the Ethics of Evil," *Ethics*, October 1945.

Parsons, Talcott. "On the Concept of Political Power." In *Proceedings of the American Philosophical Society*, vol. 107, June 1963, pp. 232-62.

Robson, William A. *The University Teaching of Social Sciences: Political Science*. Paris: United Nations Educational, Scientific, and Cultural Organization, 1954.

Rogow, Arnold A. and Harold D. Lasswell. *Power, Corruption, and Rectitude*. Englewood Cliffs, N. J.: Prentice-Hall, 1963.

Walter, E. V. "Power, Civilization, and the Psychology of Conscience." *American Political Science Review*, September 1959, pp. 641-61.

Young, Roland, ed. *Approaches to the Study of Politics*. Evanston, Ill.: Northwestern University Press, 1958.

3. Structural—Functional Analysis

Anderson, Walfred and Frederick Parker. *Society: Its Organization and Operation*. Princeton, N. J.: D. Van Nostrand, 1964.

Apter, David E. *Some Conceptual Approaches to the Study of Modernization.* Englewood Cliffs. N. J.: Prentice-Hall, 1968.

Apter, David E. and Harry Eckstein, eds. *Comparative Politics: A Reader.* New York: Free Press of Glencoe, 1963.

Beals, Alan. *Culture in Process.* New York: Holt, Rinehart and Winston, 1967.

Bentley, Arthur F. *The Process of Government.* Bloomington, Ind.: Principia Press, 1949.

Cohen, Percy S. *Modern Social Theory.* New York: Basic Books, 1968.

Darwin, Charles. *Origin of Species.* London: J. Murray, 1859.

Darwin, Charles. *Descent of Man.* London: J. Murray, 1871.

Demerath, N.J. III and Richard A. Peterson, eds. *System, Change, and Conflict.* New York: Free Press of Glencoe, 1967.

Friedrich, Carl J. *Man and His Government: An Empirical Theory of Politics.* New York: McGraw-Hill, 1963.

Hertzler, Joyce O. *Social Institutions.* Lincoln, Neb.: University of Nebraska Press, 1946.

Levy, Marion J. Jr. *The Structure of Society.* Princeton, N. J.: Princeton University Press, 1952.

Martindale, Don, ed. *Functionalism in the Social Sciences.* Philadelphia: American Academy of Political and Social Science, 1965.

Meehan, Eugene. *The Theory and Method of Political Analysis.* Homewood, Ill.: Dorsey Press, 1965.

Meehan, Eugene. *Contemporary Political Thought.* Homewood, Ill.: Dorsey Press, 1967.

Merton, Robert K. *Social Theory and Social Structure,* rev. ed. New York: Free Press of Glencoe, 1957.

Mitchell, William C. *The American Polity.* New York: Free Press of Glencoe, 1962.

Mitchell, William C. *Sociological Analysis and Politics: The Theories of Talcott Parsons.* Englewood Cliffs, N. J.: Prentice-Hall, 1967.

Nagel, Ernest. *Logic Without Metaphysics.* New York: Free Press of Glencoe, 1956.

Nettl, J. P. *Political Mobilization.* London: Faber and Faber, 1967.

Parsons, Talcott. *The Social System.* New York: Free Press of Glencoe, 1951.

Parsons, Talcott. *Structure and Process in Modern Societies.* New York: Free Press of Glencoe, 1960.

Parsons, Talcott and Gerald M. Platt. *The American University.* Cambridge, Mass.: Harvard University Press, 1973.

Radcliffe-Brown, A. R. *Structure and Function in Primitive Society.* London: Cohen and West, 1952.

Rasmussen, Jorgen. *The Process of Politics.* New York: Atherton Press, 1969.

Riddle, Donald H. and Robert E. Cleary, eds. *Political Science in the Social Studies*. Washington, D. C.: National Council for the Social Studies, 1966.

Runciman, W. G. *Social Science and Social Theory*. Cambridge: Cambridge University Press, 1963.

Truman, David B. *The Governmental Process*. New York: Knopf, 1951.

4. The Comparison of Total Political Systems

Almond, Gabriel and G. Bingham Powell, Jr. *Comparative Politics: A Developmental Approach*. Boston: Little, Brown, 1966.

Easton, David. *A Framework for Political Analysis*. Englewood Cliffs, N. J.: Prentice-Hall, 1965.

Easton, David. *A Systems Analysis of Political Life*. New York: Wiley, 1965.

Kapp, K. William. *Toward a Science of Man in Society*. The Hague: Martinus Nijhoff, 1961.

Miller, James G. "Toward a General Theory for the Behavioral Sciences," *American Psychologist,* vol. 10, 1955.

Moore, Barrington, Jr. "The New Scholasticism and the Study of Politics," *World Politics,* vol. 6, October 1953.

Wiener, Norbert. *The Human Uses of Human Beings*. New York: Doubleday-Anchor Books, 1954.

Young, Oran. *Systems of Political Science*. Englewood Cliffs, N. J.: Prentice-Hall, 1968.

5. Comparative Politics and Political Theory

Apter, David E. *The Politics of Modernization*. Chicago: University of Chicago Press, 1965.

Barber, Bernard. *Science and the Social Order*. Glencoe, Ill.: Free Press, 1952.

Barrett, William. *Irrational Man: A Study in Existential Philosophy*. New York: Doubleday, 1958.

Becker, Ernest. *The Structure of Evil: An Essay on the Justification of the Science of Man*. New York: George Braziller, 1966.

Brecht, Arnold. *Political Theory: The Foundations of Twentieth Century Political Thought*. Princeton, N. J.: Princeton University Press, 1959.

Butterfield, Herbert. *The Origins of Modern Science 1300-1800*. New York: Macmillan, 1950.

Charlesworth, James C., ed. *Mathematics and the Social Sciences: The Utility and Inutility of Mathematics in the Study of Economics, Political Science, and Sociology*. Philadelphia: American Academy of Political and Social Science, 1963.

Charlesworth, James C., ed. *A Design for Political Science: Scope, Objectives, and Methods*. Philadelphia: American Academy of Political and Social Science, 1966.

Cohen, Morris. *Reason and Nature.* Glencoe, Ill.: Free Press, 1955.

Conant, James Bryant. *Two Modes of Thought.* New York: Trident Press, 1964.

Curtis, Michael. *Comparative Government and Politics,* 2d ed. New York: Harper and Row, 1978.

Dahl, Robert A. "The Behavioral Approach in Political Science: Epitaph for a Monument to a Successful Protest." *American Political Science Review,* December 1961, pp. 763-72.

Deutsch, Karl W. *The Nerves of Government: Models of Political Communication and Control.* New York: Free Press of Glencoe, 1963.

Easton, David. "The Current Meaning of Behavioralism in Political Science." In James C. Charlesworth, ed., *The Limits of Behavioralism in Political Science.* Philadelphia: American Academy of Political and Social Science, 1962, pp. 1-25.

Ellul, Jacques. *A Critique of the New Commonplaces.* New York: Knopf, 1968.

Eulau, Heinz. "Values in Behavioral Science: Neutrality Revisited." *Antioch Review,* vol. 28, Summer 1968, pp. 160-67.

Frankl, Viktor E. *Man's Search for Meaning: An Introduction to Logotherapy.* New York: Washington Square Press, 1967.

Frohock, Fred M. *The Nature of Political Thought.* Homewood, Ill.: Dorsey Press, 1967.

Froman, Lewis A., Jr. *People and Politics: An Analysis of the American Political System.* Englewood Cliffs, N. J.: Prentice-Hall, 1962.

Germino, Dante. *Beyond Ideology: The Revival of Political Theory.* New York: Harper and Row, 1967.

Handy, Rollo. *Methodology of the Behavioral Sciences: Problems and Controversies.* Springfield, Ill.: Charles C. Thomas, 1964.

Hayek, F. A. *The Counter-Revolution of Science: Studies in the Abuse of Reason.* Glencoe, Ill.: Free Press, 1952.

Kaplan, Abraham. *The Conduct of Inquiry: Methodology for Behavioral Science.* San Francisco: Chandler, 1964.

Kateb, George. *Political Theory: Its Nature and Uses.* New York: St. Martin's Press, 1968.

Kemeny, John G. and J. Laurie Snell. *Mathematical Models in the Social Sciences.* Boston: Ginn, 1962.

Kluckhohn, Clyde. *Culture and Behavior.* New York: Free Press of Glencoe, 1962.

Lazarsfeld, Paul, ed. *Mathematical Thinking in the Social Sciences.* Glencoe, Ill.: Free Press, 1954.

Lee, Alfred McClung. *Multivalent Man.* New York: George Braziller, 1966.

McDonald, Lee C. *Western Political Theory.* New York: Harcourt, Brace, 1968.

Mannheim, Karl. *Ideology and Utopia.* New York: Harcourt, Brace, 1949.

Merriam, Charles E. *New Aspects of Politics.* Chicago: University of Chicago Press, 1925.

Mills, C. Wright. *The Sociological Imagination.* New York: Oxford University Press, 1959.

Morgenthau, Hans J. *Scientific Man vs. Power Politics.* Chicago: University of Chicago Press, 1946.

Myrdal, Gunnar. *Value in Social Theory.* London: Routledge and Kegan Paul, 1958.

Northrop, F. S. C. *The Complexity of Legal and Ethical Experience.* Boston: Little, Brown, 1959.

Polanyi, Michael. *Personal Knowledge.* Chicago: University of Chicago Press, 1958.

Rose, Arnold M. *Theory and Method in the Social Sciences.* Minneapolis: University of Minnesota Press, 1954.

Sabine, George H. *A History of Political Theory.* New York: Henry Holt, 1950.

Shils, E. A. and H. A. Finch, eds. *Max Weber on the Methodology of the Social Sciences.* Glencoe, Ill.: Free Press, 1949.

Simon, Herbert A. *Models of Man: Social and Rational.* New York: Wiley, 1957.

Smith, David G. "Political Science and Political Theory." *American Political Science Review,* September 1957, pp. 734-46.

Smith, Huston. "On Ethical Relativism." In Charles F. Madden, ed., *Talks with Social Scientists.* Carbondale, Ill.: Southern Illinois University Press, 1968, pp. 118-29.

Stein, Herman D., ed. *Social Theory and Social Invention.* Cleveland: Press of Case Western University, 1968.

Strauss, Leo. *Natural Right and History.* Chicago: University of Chicago Press, 1953.

Strauss, Leo. *What Is Political Philosophy?* Glencoe, Ill.: Free Press. 1959.

Voeglin, Eric. *The New Science of Politics.* Chicago: University of Chicago Press, 1952.

Wallas, Graham. *Human Nature in Politics.* New York: Appleton-Century Crofts, 1908.

Whitehead, Alfred North. *The Function of Reason.* Princeton, N. J.: Princeton University Press, 1929.

Wolin, Sheldon. *Politics and Vision.* Boston: Little, Brown, 1960.

Wood, Neal. "Political Behavioralism." *Commonweal,* October 4, 1968, pp. 17-22.

6. New Horizons for Comparative Politics

Banks, Arthur S. and Robert B. Textor. *A Cross-Polity Survey.* Cambridge, Mass.: M.I.T. Press, 1963.

Bill, James A. and Robert L. Hardgrave, Jr. *Comparative Politics: The Quest for Theory.* Columbus, Ohio: Charles E. Merrill, 1973.

Comparative Politics, vol. 1, no. 1, October 1968.

Downs, James F. *Cultures in Crisis.* Beverly Hills, Cal.: Glencoe Press, 1971.

Graham, George J. and George W. Carey, eds. *The Post-Behavioral Era: Perspectives on Political Science.* New York: David McKay, 1972.

Holt, Robert T. and John E. Turner. *The Methodology of Comparative Research.* New York: Free Press of Glencoe, 1970.

Inkeles, Alex and David H. Smith. *Becoming Modern: Individual Change in Six Developing Countries.* Cambridge, Mass.: Harvard University Press, 1974.

Isaak, Alan C. *Scope and Methods of Political Science.* Homewood, Ill.: Dorsey Press, 1975.

Lijphart, Arend. "Comparative Politics and the Comparative Method." *American Political Science Review,* September 1971, pp. 682-93.

Macridis, Roy C. and Bernard Brown. *Comparative Politics: Notes and Readings,* 5th ed. Homewood, Ill.: Dorsey Press, 1977.

Mayer, Lawrence C. *Comparative Political Inquiry: A Methodological Survey.* Homewood, Ill.: Dorsey Press, 1972.

Peters, Guy, John C. Doughtie, and M. Kathleen McCulloch. "Types of Democratic Systems and Types of Public Policy: An Empirical Examination." *Comparative Politics,* vol. 9, no. 3, April 1977, pp. 327-55.

Rustow, Dankwart A. "Modernization and Comparative Politics." *Comparative Politics,* vol. 1, no. 1, October 1968, pp. 37-51.

Welsh, William A. *Studying Politics.* New York: Praeger, 1973.

7. The Evaluation of Political Systems

Dahl, Robert A. "The Evaluation of Political Systems." In Ithiel de Sola Pool, ed., *Contemporary Political Science.* New York: McGraw-Hill, 1967, pp. 166-81.

Friedrich, Carl J. "Political Pathology." *Political Quarterly,* January-March 1966.

Huntington, Samuel P. *Political Order in Changing Societies.* New Haven, Conn.: Yale University Press, 1968.

Johnson, Chalmers. *Revolutionary Change.* Boston: Little, Brown, 1966.

Kautsky, J. *The Political Consequences of Modernization.* New York: Wiley, 1972.

Rostow, W. W. *Politics and the Stages of Growth.* Cambridge: Cambridge University Press, 1971.

Yartz, Frank J., Allan L. Larson, and David J. Hassel. *Progress and the Crisis of Man.* Chicago: Nelson-Hall, 1976.

Index

DATE DUE